Time's Lie

The Narrativisation of Life

Time's Lie

The Narrativisation of Life

Leo Cookman

Winchester, UK
Washington, USA

JOHN HUNT PUBLISHING

First published by Zero Books, 2020
Zero Books is an imprint of John Hunt Publishing Ltd., No. 3 East St., Alresford,
Hampshire SO24 9EE, UK
office@jhpbooks.com
www.johnhuntpublishing.com
www.zero-books.net

For distributor details and how to order please visit the 'Ordering' section on our website.

ISBN: 978 1 78904 339 6
978 1 78904 340 2 (ebook)
Library of Congress Control Number: 2019903189

A CIP catalogue record for this book is available from the British Library.

Design: Stuart Davies

UK: Printed and bound by CPI Group (UK) Ltd, Croydon, CR0 4YY
US: Printed and bound by Thomson-Shore, 7300 West Joy Road, Dexter, MI 48130

We operate a distinctive and ethical publishing philosophy in
all areas of our business, from our global network of authors to
production and worldwide distribution.

Contents

For Carrie

Acknowledgements

First and largest thanks to Doctors James Smith and Joel Swann for their continued guidance, constructive criticism, encouragement and frankly bewildering faith in my abilities, Alfie Bown for help getting feet in doors, Jared and Alec along with all the writers and the team over at Wisecrack, Philosophy Now magazine, Lou, Miles, Phillipa, Jarrod, Gus & Kitty, Abi and David for being my only close 'Writer Pals' and to Lesley, my mum, whose contribution to my writing and generally just keeping me alive is immeasurable. Finally, Thank You Carrie for your patience, enthusiasm, love and understanding, I hope our story is a good one and a long one.

Introduction

In June 2015 the President for the Spokane, WA chapter of the National Association for the Advancement of Coloured People, Rachel Dolezal, resigned after her ethnicity was questioned on camera and she walked away without answering. Dolezal's parents said she had 'disguised herself' as African American and genealogist Elizabeth Banas found she had only white ancestors over the last 4 centuries. The fallout was immediate and explosive, resulting in her dismissal from her position as Instructor in Africana Studies at Eastern Washington University, to say nothing of the viral sensation created on social media. Why did she do it? *How* did she do it? How did a person of demonstrably white heritage convince so many people she was black? Dolezal's response was simple: she self-identifies as black.

Similarly, US Senator Elizabeth Warren was challenged to take a DNA test to prove her claimed Native American heritage. While there was 'strong evidence' of Native American Ancestry, doubt was raised over the validity of Warren's claim nonetheless. Despite being raised with the family lore that they were descended from Cherokees, she could – and did – identify as white or minority when it suited her. Some say this is simply done for political point scoring, others say she is delusional, while *she* might say it is to maintain a deeper and further reaching connection to her home country. Others pointed out that the definition of her identity as Native American could not be ascertained by a simple DNA test, especially not when it was demanded by a petty and suspicious president with a history of the implicitly racist demand for 'proof of origin' from human beings. Whatever the reason and whatever the methods, the discussion would not exist if there were not differing definitions of what constitutes heritage, ancestry and even race itself.

Being in control of 'the narrative', be it your own or something

1

in the public sphere, has become a much more prominent idea in recent years. The book and movie *Gone Girl* portrays a married couple whose lives are continually moulded and reshaped by which of them is currently in control of the narrative. The public's perceptions of the couple are swayed by inconsistent evidence but with a persuasive story that ties those elements together. A more satisfying story is preferred over an objective truth, which is often messier and less appealing. This also ignores the huge irony that the movie/book itself is a narrative that the viewer/reader is also buying into. The success of this story says a lot about the world we currently live in, the 'Post Truth' society as it has been dubbed. A world where national leaders and prominent public figures can outright lie and even be confronted with their falsity but still manage to convince people they are correct, despite evidence to the contrary. Even if they themselves were recorded as saying the exact opposite of what they are currently saying, by sheer weight of conviction in their own narrative they can deny reality. But what about Dolezal and Warren? They are making direct challenges to publicly agreed upon and foundationally integral ideas of race and identity, ideas that are being manipulated to suit the individual. This results in anyone who clings to socially agreed upon facts and consensus findings being left bewildered and outraged that 'reality' can be refuted so brazenly and so successfully. Those who control the narrative are those who are in control, it seems.

I don't like the word 'narrative'. I only knew it in relation to fiction and storytelling prior to the age of 20, what with me being a writer and all. Many is the *How To Write* book I've read over the years that discusses 'narrative structure' etcetera. It's only in the last 15 years or so I have heard the word in reference to current events and real life. The more it cropped up in conversation and in media – a 'news narrative' and the like – the more I insisted on referring to things in my own writing as 'Story' in an attempt to ostracise what was fast becoming an overused word. No major event today goes undiscussed in such a global public sphere, and a quick way of aggregating the opinion or the perception of an event is to talk about its progression from start to current moment as a linear, moment-to-moment narrative. This phenomenon has been noticed and mercilessly ridiculed by comedian DaftLimmy on Twitter, who even posted a graph from Google Books of usage since 1800, revealing a huge upswing in usage since the 1980s but, as he points out, the graph only goes until 2008, prior to what feels like peak narrative discussion. And yet the term seems to be here to stay for the foreseeable future, only growing in popularity, and encapsulates this subjectivity of experience that we are all being confronted with on a daily basis, not just in the news cycle but in our own lives.

While it may seem like a bit of labelling for a topical concern, this desire to fall back on narrative when looking at events, or just simply our lives, is born out of the very way we exist day to day. We see time as a linear progression: Past to Present, Birth to Death. Time dictates our narratives. Or does it?

That phrase should really be: our *perception* of time dictates our narratives. Because – as I will be exploring in this book – time is a much more malleable product than we care to admit. There is plenty of science that reveals how little we know about time and if it even works the way we think it does, but due to the way we perceive time from birth, time informs how we see the world, how we arrange the events of our lives and consequently how narratives are created. This, I argue, is Time's Lie.

This book is an attempt to define 'narrativisation', or the method by which we create and impose narratives on events, and to refute the belief that narratives somehow simply 'emerge' as it is sometimes claimed – 'a new narrative has emerged' being a frequent New Media buzzword – by looking at what a story is, how narrative is constructed and why it is we tell ourselves these stories anyway.

Part 1

Story

Chapter 1

Campfire Tales

'Stories are wild creatures' explains the titular Monster from the Patrick Ness novel *A Monster Calls*, and it isn't wrong. As anyone who knows the truth behind a rumour or has played the game Chinese Whispers will understand, a story quickly develops, grows and changes from inception to reception. They are, as the Monster suggests, untameable. And yet we tell stories every day, to ourselves, to others, in conversation, in emails, true and 'embellished', honest or otherwise. Not a day goes by without a tale being told. Story creation is ingrained into our very DNA. We will explore the practical implications of this later in the book, but for now it will help us to look back at how we have told stories in the past and how those stories, and methods of telling them, have evolved.

Story and narrative are often treated as interchangeable terms, but for our purposes it would be helpful to make them distinct. A narrative is the connective element of events when those events are related as a story. Russian Formalists defined this as fabula and syuzhet, fabula being the specifics of what happened, while syuzhet is the formation of those elements into some sort of recognisable order. A story, then, is the object, the 'thing', that the narrative lives inside. And be assured, narratives are definitely 'alive'. A good short-hand is to look at film credits. The *Star Wars* sequel *The Empire Strikes Back* credits Leigh Brackett and Lawrence Kasdan as the screenplay writers but there is also a story credit that belongs to George Lucas, meaning that Lucas made the story, Kasdan and Brackett wrote the narrative. A story can be summarised, it can be described with adjectives that have emotional connotations. 'A sad and affecting story' you might say of Romeo and Juliet. It is rare you would describe a narrative that way. You might say a narrative was 'interesting' or 'difficult' but not 'sweet' or as a 'Love' narrative. A story is almost always considered fiction too, a narrative is just the facts, a retelling of events, whether the tale is fiction or not. This creates the contradiction that a story is the object but described in subjective terms, whereas the narrative is always subjective (relating a narrative accurately/correctly is dependent on the author or narrator) but described in objective terms. Despite these distinctions they are inextricably linked: there is no story without a narrative and there can be no narrative without a story. But if there can be no narrative without a story, then why should we look at real life as a narrative, as our life doesn't abide by a 'story' as we have just defined it? I would argue: it does.

History itself has a narrative, that of past to present. Despite many efforts to write an 'Entire History of the World', that would prove an impossible (and pointless) task if you were to *literally* write the entire history of the world, so historians tend to package elements of history into more succinct narratives i.e. stories. This method is as old as humanity itself. Before written language, we have cave paintings that show us, in their most rudimentary forms, a type of narrative, showing us what events or objects were deemed significant to our ancestors. Even after written language was developed but before literacy was more commonplace, we know an oral history was kept. These storytellers were the eldest of a tribe who in turn had been told the history of their people by *their* elders and so on. It was in these types of 'histories' that the most basic forms of narrative structures developed: the beginning, the middle and the end. It is unlikely early man gave lectures on narrative design but out of necessity when telling a story of any kind you start at a beginning and you eventually end it. Like the metaphorical piece of string, you and I may cut it in a different place, but we always still cut a length from the whole, you don't use an entire ball of string every time you want to tie something up. It is in these original storytellers that we can see the story as object. The story was a precious and guarded thing, kept and treasured by the storyteller; the narrative is the means of delivery.

It is important to note here the communal aspect of stories. The Classical Greeks understood this best. 'To the Greeks, spoken word was a living thing and infinitely preferable to the dead symbols of written language,' according to Eugene and Margaret Bahn in *A History of Oral Interpretation*. This can be seen in the Greek tragedies and comedies that told the history of Greece but also made them performative, dramatic and enjoyable to an audience. We wouldn't have those huge ancient amphitheatres if there were not stories to tell and people who wanted to hear them. Aristotle believed one of the reasons for theatre's success specifically was that their narratives produced an effect he called catharsis, the act of purification or of purging an emotion. By going to see theatre, the audience was engaged in the act of catharsis through the symbolism of the play, a belief that is born out in contemporary psychological research. For this reason and more, stories command attention, whether in a theatre or not. We will happily sit/stand around the metaphorical campfire and listen to the storyteller impart his tale. Even if today it's a watercooler and Gary from accounting telling an anecdote with vaguely sexist overtones. The point being, a story is a shared experience. We enjoy it (or not) and it is logged in the collective memory. 'You know that story!' we will say. Just like the Ancient Greeks this method of telling and retelling stories keeps the story not just alive but living. Which, conveniently, brings us back to those wild creatures.

When a story is told, it is given. The object is handed over. So we know the story, we have it in our hands, as it were, but the narrative? That's up for debate.

'There were fifteen of them!'
'You said it was five before...'

It's a comic cliché for a reason. The story will often stay the same but whether deliberately embellished or simply misremembered, the details alter, thus so does the narrative and that wild creature begins to quickly wriggle free from your grasp. Consequently, any history we tell is unreliable, or at least not totally accurate to the actual events as they happened. Skilled historians will find supporting evidence, other accounts, images, that will help to corroborate the story but ultimately they must acknowledge that their account will only ever be partial, their declarations provisional. They are trying to get the narratives to align, but due to the fact narratives, by their very nature, must compress the events and so leave out certain details, a historian must fill in those blanks and is, therefore, still writing their own narrative to fit the story.

While 'history is never 100 per cent accurate' is probably page one of the 'Historian's Manual' and must be treated with great care to avoid the unpleasant, reactionary side of that statement that creates deniers of history, it is worth establishing these ideas as they will be useful in discussions later in this book. The idea that we tend to tell the story of Hitler's rise to power, or the story of the Renaissance, without necessarily exploring the hundreds of other narratives around the world that either directly or indirectly contributed to those stories is an indicator of how more specific narratives are so influential to us as a species. These are stories plucked from the whole. They may be used as supporting narratives elsewhere, it's true, but they are still singular objects to be related, revised and retold. And because they are stories, we tell them in a certain way. No story about Hitler is complete without, say, explaining the Munich Agreement. No relating of the story of the Renaissance is complete without Da Vinci. We still apply plot points i.e. narrative elements, to our histories. Our lives are not lived to add 'character beats' or 'moments of exposition', our lives do not have a theme or a subtext necessarily, but the fact these elements are integral to storytelling says something about how important similar events are in our lives. Life dictates story and story dictates life, while the narrative is how this is all pieced together.

Today we hold storytellers in the same high regard as we once did all those millennia ago. We still flock to the cinema, or read the latest bestseller, or listen to the newsreader, or watch the scientist that's a talking head in a documentary who gathers all those fantastic pieces of physics together to explain a phenomenon we previously knew nothing about. And we all have that friend too, don't we? The one who can make a trip to get a bottle of milk a hilarious cavalcade of mishaps and thrills, the raconteur, the wit. Boy do we love those people. Whether we consider it scientific fact, historical data, mass market fiction or just an anecdote from Gary in the office, it's all fundamentally just a story.

Chapter 2

Ripping Yarns

No discussion of story would be complete without investigating its most overt form: the Lie. A lie, in its simplest terms, is a story that the person relating knows is untrue, but the person listening does not. If the person listening *does* know it is false, then that is simply fiction. Immediately, though, we run into problems with that definition. As discussed in the previous chapter, stories are wild things, living things, that resist being exactly defined. Try as we might with written language or cinema or fine art, we cannot make a story the metaphorical butterfly on display, pinned down for all to admire in its perfection. As TS Eliot wrote in *The Love Song of J. Alfred Prufrock*:

> *When I am pinned and wriggling on the wall,*
> *Then how should I begin*
> *To spit out all the butt ends of my days and ways?*

Every story continues to wriggle and dance in its display case. We can all leave the cinema, turn off a newscast or put down the same book and have entirely different understandings or interpretations of the story, whether it was presented as fact or not. We will come to how this occurs through perspective and meaning later in this book but for now we must recognise that the story, the wild creature it is, will always resist capture. This is where narrative asserts its importance.

Narrative creates consistency. As an example, let's look at a story and its narrative. The story is that of Christ sacrificing himself on the cross for mankind's collective sins; the narrative is that Judas betrays him after the Last Supper and he is caught and imprisoned, then led through the streets of Jerusalem carrying a wooden cross that he is then crucified upon under the orders of Pontius Pilate. Ask most people who live in a historically Christian or Catholic country and you'll get some vaguely similar answers about the events around Jesus' death (and *even then*, this comes from four Gospels that emphasise different elements of this narrative). We can, however, point to this narrative consistency as a form of consensus about the events that lead to his death, even if it is all from one (questionable) source. It's also worth noting that there is a consensus in historical research that Jesus of Nazareth did actually exist. Consistency and consensus can at least make some of this story seem true to the point we can assert Jesus' existence as fact...then we see the butterfly wriggle.

For some this story is – quite literally – gospel, for others, it's not. For many the 'fault' in this story lies with different people and groups and without getting into the protracted and often vile interpretations of who did what to whom and why, this example shows how malleable a story's narrative and its meaning can be even if we *agree* the events did actually happen. A lie on the other hand – that I am the greatest ballerina of our age, for instance – is a story, and I can even give you the narrative to back it up. Here:

> I always loved ballet since I saw Prokofiev's *Romeo and Juliet* performed at the Marlowe Theatre in Canterbury when I was ten. After years of athletics and successes in regional competitions I began ballet classes despite the stigma associated with a 13-year-old boy joining a ballet school. I excelled at the Deborah Capon dance school and was cast centrally throughout my developing years, but my real break came when I went to university to study movement at...oh but I won't bore you.

Now, if you were to watch a video of my entire life and saw everything I ever did and said, you will find that I did indeed see Prokofiev's *Romeo and Juliet* at the Marlowe. The wonderful, and sadly late, Deborah Capon was a local legend and ran her nationally recognised ballet school in my home town. These facts, while true, did not add up to me being the prima ballerina of the Northern Ballet, I am sorry to say. But I could have evidence to support this if I really wanted to convince you. I still possess the programme for that performance at the Marlowe, I have many friends who were alumni of the ballet school I could introduce you to, I could talk for quite a while on why Sergei Polunin is one of the all-time greats. All the elements and more are there. We have the narrative, a false one, but it supports the story and, even if I do say so myself, I can be pretty convincing when I want to be. Where I'd come unstuck is consistency: 'You said *years* in athletics, yet you saw Prokofiev at 10 then attended ballet school at 13. So just three years? And isn't 13 a little late of a start for a great ballet artist?' If I were in the mood (and you'd had a few) I could clarify, 'I misspoke' blah blah blah and you might even believe me. It certainly isn't outside the realms of possibility. It is a believable story and it has narrative supporting proofs. Then the butterfly begins to wriggle.

The lie is revealed when there is no consensus. There is not a consistency of narrative. Check the records, no Leo Cookman went to Deborah's school, those costumes were from amateur dramatics plays I was in, those friends from the ballet school I met at the theatre I used to perform at, but as an actor not a dancer. If we introduce other narratives the story falls apart. By contrast if I had said, 'I'm going to tell you a story about a boy who grew up to be the greatest dancer of his generation,' and presented it as fiction, the very facts that blew apart my lie would only strengthen a fiction. I know more than the average Joe about ballet because of the reasons listed above and those facts become narrative elements that better the story. The fiction story *purely because of its lack of consistency* is able to be adopted and adapted by others and, counterintuitively, ends up containing more truth than it would have had I presented it as true. As Plato once commented, 'Poetry is nearer to vital truth than history.'

Let us be clear, while a lie in this context shares many of its attributes with the truth, it is not the truth. Falsity is correctly despised and shunned by society at large. Dishonesty is and always should be a negative trait. So why have lies become not only permissible but accepted today? Many of us watch in horror as the latest celebrity or politician is caught contradicting themselves but they merely brush this off and it is not pursued. Or when they make a provably untrue statement that they, even when presented with the facts, persist with. This is now a daily occurrence in the media which puts us in the depressing situation where these lies then propagate themselves. And why wouldn't they? If someone is on a previously trusted television network or in a broadsheet publication, why wouldn't you believe what they say? We have so far, after all.

Again, a story is an object. It can be true or untrue, but it is always created by us. The context in which the story is told, and the consensus and consistency of the narrative is what makes it true or untrue. These lies are presented to us in the context of truth, by figures of power and respect, on television networks and media outlets that purport to present facts, and because of that a consensus is called for, even if the consistency of the narrative is dubious. Simply by presenting the story as true, others will bring their own narratives (prejudices or biases would be another word) to it and create a false consistency. For example, one of the most popular (and in my mind most reprehensible) narratives that has been created in recent times is that of immigration. The famous 'They come over here and take our jobs' narrative that has been created is laughably false yet persists in the everyday 'concerns over immigration' people supposedly have. That last sentence alone would draw ire from some people, stating the horrors of immigration are a stone-cold fact, they know, they've seen it! They will tell you about their friend, or even an anecdote about themselves, where a foreign worker undercut them, replaced them in their work, or simply a foreign labourer turned up to fix something in their house. Despite the fact this is tangential and anecdotal information, or that evidence suggests it is the employers who create this issue by cutting wages to a point that domestic workers are, rightfully, unwilling to accept, or that it shows an *astounding* level of entitlement to demand that it was 'your' job to begin with, none of this is relevant to this person who demands a 'conversation about immigration' because *none of it is consistent with their narrative*. A narrative built up over their lifetime and based on their experience. They may not even have any hard evidence or anecdotes to back up their belief, but the narrative presented to them *feels* true and correct. What Arlie Russell Hochschild referred to as the 'Deep Story'. The more people that add to the narrative of immigration the more consistent it becomes, the larger the consensus, until finally, it is the 'Truth'.

Liberals and those on the Left were horrified at Trump's success in the 2016 election, as was I. My partner is American, and I was visiting the States during the election. I was convinced Trump would not get the required votes. How wrong I was. More than a few tears were shed that night, I can tell you. I was also living in the left-wing, Green MP bubble of Brighton during the EU Referendum. That time, however, I foresaw the outcome. I grew up in a Conservative constituency not far from the far-Right party UKIP controlled council of Thanet and one of their only two constituency seats in Rochester and Strood. Because of that I was more than aware of the gripes over immigration, work, the NHS, etc, that were being pandered to by the Leave campaign and how strongly they were felt. The general consensus, however, seemed to be we would remain in the EU.

The butterfly wriggled.

But how? The discussion still continues to this day and there are many, many narratives about how and why these, to some catastrophic, to others transformative, events happened. The argument I am making is that it is precisely because the stories of Trump and Brexit were presented by institutions of honesty and respect, be that in a positive or negative light, that the invented narratives of 'He's not a politician, he's going to drain the swamp' and 'We're going to get our country back' could gain purchase despite being utterly false and based on no plausible evidence. The stories were told to a huge range of people, some of whom shared many of the narrative elements they were asked to believe, and the wriggle room of narrative was able to accommodate them. The narratives themselves, both seeming to conform to a type of 'Make America/Britain Great Again' mentality, are complex and multifarious but the fact is the narratives are what sold the story and the narrative became more consistent the more people contributed to it.

Far from saying all narratives are lies, or that all narratives are true, I am saying all narratives can be considered either and we are seeing the repercussions of that. A wild creature is neither good nor bad, it just is. We dictate whether it is wild enough or too wild, the creature just does what it wants. This is why we have to be careful with not only how we create a story but how we present the story because it is at these junctures that narrative is created, the heart of the story starts beating, and if we do not present the story correctly immediately, or train the creature straight away, we lose our grip on it and it takes on a life of its own. Roland Barthes describes a similar idea in his essay *La mort de l'auteur,* that once the author has released their work it is no longer theirs, it is subject to the vagaries of public opinion. As soon as a story is presented it takes a lot to control it thereafter. As soon as Trump was presented as a possible candidate, it was all over. As soon as the Referendum was offered, it was too late. The wild creature was released. The butterfly wriggled free.

A note on jokes:

Jokes can be considered narratives but a very special kind

of narrative for they have no ending. Hannah Gadsby in her exceptional show 'Nanette' makes the point that a joke has no closure. Her moving example of this is how she used to tell a joke in her previous show about being mistaken for a man when flirting with a woman because of her masculine appearance. Realising his mistake, the man backs away. It's a funny bit. Sadly, it's only half the story, half the narrative, only half true. In reality, that man caught up with her after she left and beat her until she was hospitalised. That's...less funny.

A joke is a setup and then a twist. 'A Dyslexic man walked into a bra', as an example, reveals how we abandon the man at the twist because the joke is fulfilled. No more narrative required. This works if you want a laugh, but abandoning the narrative at the twist in a movie, immediately rolling the credits at the moment we realise 'whodunnit' for instance, would be deeply unsatisfying.

Trump's running for president was considered a joke. We didn't abandon him at that moment.

Chapter 3

Heroes as Heroin

My favourite books on the topic of writing were written by the late William Goldman but there are thousands of others to choose from, all associated with different elements of writing and in different styles. There is one text, however, that stands above all others and has moved far beyond the shallow enclave of fiction writers it was intended for and into the public consciousness: Joseph Campbell's *The Hero with a Thousand Faces*. In it, Campbell describes what he calls the 'Monomyth', a narrative structure that is inherent to all stories. He takes this idea from various studies of myth, particularly Carl Jung's, and incorporates into his definition many of Jung's ideas about archetypes and symbolism. Jung's brand of hermeneutics has become increasingly adopted in today's world because of its ability to be used to decode almost everything. We will come to how a fascist sympathising psychoanalyst's model for understanding texts has influenced the rise of certain contemporary thinkers and their followers later but for now, understanding that Campbell was so influenced by this study of symbolism and semiotics is important. The main reason his book became so popular is because it was used by numerous writers as a method of planning a story, in particular George Lucas used it as a basis for *Star Wars*. *The Hero with a Thousand Faces* is still considered the bible for a lot of screenwriters to this day. It is also a load of hooey.

The monomyth is an attempt to flatten culture. As we have already discussed, once created narratives achieve greater consistency the greater the consensus around the narrative is. Campbell misconstrues commonality for consistency. The 'Hero's Journey', as his monomythic narrative structure has come to be called, is so common because it describes something we all go through, a journey, and then things that happen along the way, a la the oldest European narrative we have on record, *The Odyssey*. If his definition had been this broad, I would understand, but he introduces 17 very specific stages for the narrative to work through: the call to adventure, the refusal of the call, meeting the mentor, etc. Sounding familiar? This is essentially to be used as a method of breeding the same not-very-wild creature over and over again. And breed it did.

Look up the 17 stages online and you will begin to see the pattern emerge. Countless books, TV shows, movies, anecdotes, histories and, yes, myths follow this formula. If you are new to the theory, it is an amazing discovery. You can effortlessly decode even the most convoluted narrative by following these 17 steps. An abundance of video essays on YouTube do just that, in fact, for almost every major cinema, TV or book release. Yet despite its purported 'detail', this is as broad and as ambiguous a methodology as simply stating all stories have a beginning, middle and end. Yes, it is accurate, but it also doesn't really add anything. Books, television, comics, cinema; these things aren't getting better and better thanks to this understanding of narrative; if anything, it is those that are overusing this template that are stagnating. Furthermore, it's not generally something you're aware of or thinking about when writing or telling a story. To misquote a show that uses the Hero's Journey narrative as a template for each of its episodes, 'that's just a story with extra steps' (*Rick and Morty*). The monomyth utilises events that occur in all our lives, that we look back on as being significant, collects them and then attempts to cram every single one into a story. It is an attempt to create a formula from the messy narratives of our lives and history, which has a cheapening effect. It *works*, but it certainly cheapens the value of the story. There is nuance in the events of our lives, multiple interpretations, just like in writing fiction, and the monomyth, while serviceable, does not account for that.

The biggest problem I have with the monomyth is in its titling of the main characters. We are, none of us, heroes. There is a far better name for the central individual of a narrative and that is a 'protagonist'. A hero implies greatness, great deeds, great emotions, great speech. Odysseus would have seemed less great a champion if we saw him going to the toilet in *The Odyssey*, I'm sure. Protagonist implies only that the character is central to the narrative, the 'first combatant' as the title literally translates. It is precisely this hysterical nature surrounding the lead character that Campbell's formula attempts to create, and, as stated, it works. Look to any mass fiction today, particularly the pervasive 'comic-book culture', and you will see this narrative formula in action, but it is this standardisation that has fed into real life. Now we must all be the hero of our own journey. George W. Bush declared in true heroic fashion that 'we must fight these evil ones' after 9/11, while Reagan adopted *Star Wars* as the nomenclature for his ICBM program, both world leaders adopting the language and developing a narrative of heroism to accompany their subsequent slide into militarism. The more heroes we demand, the more they announce themselves, be that in fiction or real life.

Refuting this idea of a grand narrative does put me at odds with certain theorists, however. Francis Fukuyama, adapting a widely disputed theory by Marx, believed in the 'March of History', the narrative that humanity since inception is progressing towards a proposed 'End of History', based on Hegel's theory of dialectics. Fukuyama's book *The End of History and the Last Man* was written in 1992 when it was believed we had indeed reached the end of history, the 1990s being a period of relative prosperity for the majority of white, English-speaking nations. The rude awakening of the twenty-first century and 9/11 quickly did away with this idea and was then followed not long after by the 2008 crash. These events and those since have somewhat disabused beliefs of a grand, central narrative to our existence. Despite that, there is still *a* narrative at work and a compelling one at that. In many ways it is no different than how anyone selects a story from history or *about* history and builds the narrative to tell it, but what Hegel and Marx did that is so different to these ideas was that their narrative *projected into the future*. We will be looking at how we understand this and how this effects narrative later in this book but the reason why today the idea of history as an inevitable march of progress seems so hard to swallow is that it is able to predict as much as it reflects. Given the uncertainty of modern times, you can see why prediction – its accuracy not withstanding – has become a boom industry.

Another problem with Campbell, Fukuyama and Marx's reflections on narrative is a cultural one. None of them account for narratives as they are constructed elsewhere in the world. By necessity Japanese narratives are very different to European ones, which in turn are different to Ugandan ones and so on. Placing a definitive structure on story and narrative at a global scale removes any flexibility within a given culture. It encases the butterfly in resin, locks the wild creature in a cage, and says 'here, this is it and this is all there is'. The colours of the wings or the leopards' spots may change but they're still all the same breed. The subjectivity of narrative is its defining feature. The *story* can perhaps be more readily accepted – I agree with Marx in general, for instance, in the same way as I rather like the original *Star Wars* movies – but the narrative must be allowed to be supported by other narratives so that the all-important consensus can be arrived at. A global consensus is harder to achieve given the environmental factors that contribute to narratives. Culture is just as much a narrative as anything else because it is consistent with the experiences and narratives of those who live within it. 'Culture clashes' then could be described as 'narrative dissonance' between people. Therefore, a singular, international, catch-all story for all people does not allow for that wriggling we require from narrative.

You can see today how we try to break free from these supposedly hard and fast rules of the grand narratives and monomyths. There is a reason episodic, serial storytelling has been so popular. This 'Golden Age of Television', as it has been dubbed, allows for a wider and broader scope and for stories to be told in different ways and for different people. But there is still intense criticism for those that buck the trend. Stories and narratives that don't adhere to current fashions in fiction that have been so well established are lambasted. For instance, some of the most popular blockbuster movies in recent years (*Jurassic World: Fallen Kingdom, Batman vs Superman, Star Wars: The Last Jedi*) were all criticised for – among other things – their choices in plotting and how their story progressed. The errors in these films are more than simply their story and I do not feel the criticism that they deviated from story format is as valid as criticisms over, say, performance, direction or any other technical aspect of their production. I also do not agree stories should be without some form of narrative progression, but the current method has become formulaic to the point where 'everyone's a critic' purely by virtue of having been given the cheat-sheet. Narrative discussion is something I am keen to promote given its modern rise, but critical analysis of narrative based on hard and fast rules established in the 1940s seems reductive.

This modern trend for blockbuster over-analysis indirectly asks why are we so attached to the hero and his (and rest assured, despite contemporary changes, it is almost always a he) journey? The constant emphasis on heroes in our narratives, and not simply protagonists, has created a desire for these types of characters in real life and not just our fiction. They are great, they are good, they do what must be done, they are idolised and worshipped. The more someone presents themselves as this Jungian Archetype, the more a public, with a loosely defined set of parameters for one, will see them as such. The quality of the individual need not matter either due to the malleable nature of the hero and our ability to see past their character flaws and innate human failings when they triumph in the end. The simplistic nature and lack of nuance that is baked into the Hero's Journey can only ever result in failure at worst or misrepresentation at best. This insistence on requiring heroes will only ever lead to more Trumps.

So far, we have been looking at the why and how of narrativisation and its history. In the next section we will be looking at what a narrative is at a fundamental level and where this inherent need for narrativisation comes from.

Part 2

Time

.

Chapter 1

The Lie of Time

Here's a pretty standard narrative to begin with: I pick up a pristine crystal champagne flute, I hurl it at the cold, concrete ground, where it shatters into thousands of miniscule shards that tiptoe away from the centre of the impact. It's brief but you have basic elements of a story there, it even has a beginning, middle and an end. What it illustrates is how reliant on time the narrative is. If you reorder any of the moments in that story people will wonder why I picked up the shattered remains of a champagne flute, threw them to the floor and created a whole glass. Once you had understood the problem you would automatically reorder the sequence of events to make a logical sense. Here we see the central rule of narrative: progression. There is a term in physics for the way we perceive this linear progression of events: Time's Arrow.

The physical process that is being referred to when we talk about Time's Arrow and the linear progression of events is known as entropy. This is technically defined as the 'thermodynamic quantity representing the unavailability of a system's thermal energy for conversion into mechanical work', but it is most commonly used to describe the lack of order or randomness, and therefore gradual decline, of the universe and systems within it. A good way of understanding entropy is to look at that champagne glass again. In its current shattered state, its constituent parts i.e. the molecules and atoms that make up the glass, are in a state of high entropy. You could pick up the shattered material with a dustpan and brush and they would not form a receptacle for drinking again; they would simply get shuffled around and once they are thrown in the bin those particles would remain at rest and still in a high state of entropy. The other crystal champagne flute that was stood next to the now broken one on the table remains in a low state of entropy, due to the way the constituent particles were arranged to form the beautifully patterned glass and how static they remain. However, due to the way entropy is bound to increase in any given system thanks to it being part of the Laws of Thermodynamics, if I were to leave that glass exactly where it was, sat atop that table indefinitely, left to the elements as the building around it rotted and exposed it; the weather, the wind, the rain and falling debris from the collapsing roof would, over time, increase the glass's state of entropy. Eventually it would end up in the same state as the one I threw to the ground and shattered all those years ago.

All of this is to say that, scientifically speaking, there is a reason you can't make an omelette without breaking some eggs. The broken egg shells have a high state of entropy, as does the sizzling albumen and egg white on the frying pan, and they cannot be reversed. And it is this changing of states that we have assigned a meaning to. We call this mode of entropy 'time'. Beyond that, we have created meaning in its advance and given that process more nuanced names too, like 'decay' or 'age'. This is all in service to the way our consciousness works and how we perceive entropy. That may seem a little hard to grasp or easy to dispute but if we take a small step outside Earth and the rules that govern it, we can begin to see what happens to entropy if we separate the causal agents.

Einstein's Theory of General Relativity is sort of like the 'Pop Hit' of the physics world, despite its complexity we generally all know what it means and how it is applied i.e. that time is relative to observers in uniform motion. Essentially: time is relative to those experiencing it. On Earth humans are all moving at the same speed – the Earth's – and therefore entropy and the causal events that follow it are *so* uniform and consistent we have called it time and we run our lives by it. Even going so far as to divide it into incremental units of measurement: seconds, minutes, hours, etc. However, just by sending satellites into our orbit and matching those units of measurement exactly, we have noticed time is not consistent once you leave the uniform motion of Earth. Time's consistency is directly affected by the change in gravity. In short, entropy does not progress as consistently as we think once we have removed it from the 'Lab Conditions' of Earth. Out in the cosmos, among the stars, nebulae, black holes and quasars, our idea of time becomes even more malleable and, as we now understand it, inextricably linked with the area you are in (in our case Earth), hence Einstein linking the two by giving them the title of 'spacetime'. Due to this connection we can better understand gravity's effect on time thanks to the more easily measurable effects of gravity on space and physical objects. Gravity effects objects i.e. Particles, it is the interaction of particles that creates entropy, therefore gravity effects entropy, time is how we measure entropy, therefore gravity effects time. For the purposes of our discussion on narrative, you can see how these elements can already be used to disrupt our natural inclination towards a logical progression of events.

If you were to zoom out further than the universe even, outside our space and time, according to Edward Witten's M-Theory you could observe space and time as a single object, akin to Rust Cohle's 'Flat Circle' in True Detective. If that were the case, from the outside, an observer would see all time happening at once, and that champagne glass is, both still a drinking glass and shattered on the floor. And still the raw silica particles it was made from. And every other state the matter that constitutes that glass has been in throughout all time. This is what is known as matter being seen in its 'Superposition'.

The consistent and linear notion of Time's Arrow, therefore, is not the indefatigable law of the universe we might think. And yet, because we live on Earth and entropy has generally consistent properties within our spacetime, it's safe to just go with the trajectory Time's Arrow offers us, right? It turns out, maybe not, no. Even here, with us all in the uniform motion of Earth, how we perceive time is still under some intense philosophical debate, thanks largely to JME McTaggart's A-Theory and B-Theory of time.

The A-Theory of time states that time is divisible into the three generally accepted states of past, present and future and that objects and events have the temporal properties we associate with them. For instance, the unbroken champagne glass, before I threw it to the ground, has the property of 'Pastness', while in its freshly shattered state it has the property of 'Presentness', while the second champagne glass succumbing to the vagaries of the elements until finally shattering among the rubble of the building around it has the property of 'Futurity'. B-Theory on the other hand states that all times are equal, that Superposition again, which marries up well with the idea of spacetime. This says that time is like space in that there is no property of 'here' when it comes to space, it is just where *you* are. As such, there is no 'now' in time, it's just the name of the point in time where we happen to be, and all times exist equally. The problem with B-Theory, according to McTaggart, is that it does not account for change. In A-Theory the champagne glass *was* whole and has *become* broken, its 'wholeness' changed. The moment it was whole moved from the present and into the past, whereas if B-Theory were correct, that change couldn't happen. The glass is still whole but is in an 'earlier than' relationship with its broken state. This isn't change though, this is a form of description similar to saying 'I am stood here, not over there.' It's true but the two statements don't relate to each other and don't describe change. So, therefore, A-Theory is the way to go, right? Obviously, events move from the future into the present and then into the past? Again, according to McTaggart, no.

We generally all see time as moving like A-Theory describes it, but that method is inherently contradictory according to something called McTaggart's Paradox. This points out that this description of time that says the champagne glass has properties of pastness, presentness and futurity is a contradiction, because this way the glass only has these temporal properties based on the temporal position of the observer. To simplify, we describe that unbroken champagne glass I left on the table that degrades with the building around it over the course of years, from a present temporal position i.e. now. This means we describe it by saying 'the glass WILL shatter', giving the statement, and therefore the object and event, the temporal property of 'Present-Futurity'. That other champagne glass I threw to the ground? That WAS whole, giving that statement the temporal property of 'Present-Pastness'. This is known as describing things with 'Second Order Temporal Properties' which, as you may be able to predict, contradict each other. Perhaps you say 'alright, something may have the property of Present-Futureness' but then it moves into the past, so now it has the property of Present-Pastness. Again though, that's a contradiction, because now you're describing the champagne glass in its low entropy state before I threw it, as having Present-Future-Pastness. And in case you hadn't guessed, this can go on and on. Objects and events can have Past-Future-Past-Presentness and Present-Past-Future-Pastness, meaning they can possess third and fourth order temporal properties, fifth order properties, sixth, ad infinitum. And if you're still following along, congratulations.

The reason this becomes so complicated so quickly is because we're using time to describe time, which is what creates the Paradox. McTaggart developed A and B Theory over 100 years ago and it is broadly still the basis for most theoretical debate about time. Ultimately, you're an A Theorist or a B Theorist, both of which have sub-schools to them today but they're a good way of understanding how we perceive time and how we relate to it. And an excellent way of describing the inherent contradictions of time itself.

All of this is to say, time isn't really as straight and true as that arrow. The stories we tell, however, conform to the logical temporal order as we see it from day to day. Tomorrow is the future, today is the present, yesterday is the past. That's as much as any of us will ever experience and therefore that's all we need to tell our story. It will happen, it is happening, it happened. I will break the glass, I'm breaking the glass, the glass is broken. But that's the lie. Time doesn't conform to these descriptors we place upon it and entropy, by its very nature, is unpredictable and chaotic; neither of these properties of the universe present themselves as naturally occurring narratives or adhering to a logical sequence of events. Referring back again to TS Eliot's poem:

Do I dare
Disturb the universe?
In a minute there is time
For decisions and revisions which a minute will reverse

We will be exploring how our perception and our conscious minds create narratives later in the book but, in the next chapter, we will see how our unconscious mind is in fact better attuned to the universe's more abstract and non-linear movement of time than we generally think.

Chapter 2

Bed Time

No one likes hearing about someone else's dreams. A dream is generally only important to the person who dreamed it, mainly because it is created entirely in your own head and is more to do with the feelings it conjures up than the story it tells. Bear with me though, there's a reason for me telling you this one:

I was in some sort of lab. It looked like something out of a horror movie or videogame where there are cells or experimentation chambers lining a corridor. All crystal white walls brightly lit by halogen bulbs. Inside one of these cells was a man observing something through a two-way mirror. Beyond the two-way mirror was a blackness I could not see into. The man clearly did not want me in the room and he tried to throw me out. An altercation ensued whereupon the man in the cell pulled a short-blade pocket knife and stabbed me in the right side of my belly. Thinking me mortally wounded, the man let me go as I staggered away bleeding. I fled, and I made it out of the laboratory area where I bumped into my good friend who saw I was injured and tended to me. I explained what happened to him and he looked me dead in the eye and said, 'We have to kill him.' I agreed (it felt like the right thing to do at the time), so we turned around and made our way back into the laboratory. There we found the same cell with the same man but this time beyond the glass I could now see the bud of a giant white lily which – in an image I will take to my grave – exploded from bud into bloom, its petals curling backwards and stems vibrating in the air, pollen showering outward, but shooting out from inside it was a crystal white sperm whale that floated off into the darkness of the tank. I was drawn away from this surreal but majestic sight by my friend doing battle with the lab technician.

I went to help and wrest the blade from my attacker. As I did, I sustained another stabbing from the knife but this time, with two of us, we were able to overpower the man and it is around then the dream tails off. I'm not sure how it ended but I assume we murdered the man in cold blood. Delightful.

Like all dreams, it was pretty bloody weird and makes little-to-no logical sense. In anticipation of some obvious questions: no, I don't know who the lab technician was and no I have never had any inclination to kill anyone, nor has my friend (to the best of my knowledge). Two things have stuck with me from that dream, though: the whale bursting from the flower and being stabbed. In the context of the dream, the whale and the lily were entirely separate from the events in the lab, the incredible image was like a pocket scene of brilliantly white objects against a pitch-black back drop that bore no relation to the rest of what happened. The stabbings felt real, I remember vividly the feeling of flesh parting as the blade sliced me open, like cutting raw chicken. My memory is fuzzy, but the second stabbing happened to my hand as I tried to wrestle the weapon from my attacker's grasp. What is most interesting about my retelling of this is that, in all likelihood, those two stabbings were probably one stabbing and happened at the same time while I was dreaming, or were the same thought, but my mind separated them into two distinct events upon waking in an attempt to arrange a narrative out of the dream.

Two almost identical events separated by time in a piece of fiction is called foreshadowing but, in a dream, we have no need for thematic or structural devices like this. The two stabbings were either the same event but reordered upon waking, or two distinct stabbings that weren't in any logical order anyway that my mind then placed one after the other. Essentially, I built the narrative after it all happened, processes that Freud referred to as 'condensation' and 'displacement' in his interpretation of dreams.

This is a lot like a method of data tracking in computer coding called 'Eventual Consistency'. When looking at a popular Tweet or a YouTube video, the number of views/retweets/likes can go up AND down, this is because the sheer volume of incoming requests for a 'viral' post can overwhelm a database. To deal with this, the requests are sent to a cache where the requests are stored and then when the popularity of the post, and consequently the number of requests sent, dies down the information can be transferred to a database and you will *eventually* reach a *consistent* result. The events in your dream happen at the same time – just like those data requests – but they are cached into your memory and then sorted into a more consistent narrative later upon waking.

This reflects what we talked about in the first chapter of this section about how events and the order they happen in are not necessarily sequential or fixed, but it is how we perceive the events that creates the Future to Present to Past passage of time we adhere to in daily life. Dreams are not about a narrative, they are – by necessity – not a story to be told, which is why we never want to hear about someone else's dream and, when we do, find them so dull. There is no narrative cohesion, the person telling it has arranged the events of the dream into some sort of understandable progression of events, but it never imparts the key element of a dream to the listener: the Emotion.

Explaining the narrative of the dream is futile because your subconscious mind did not conjure a narrative, it conjured a set of images and emotions. Whether you believe a dream means anything or not, the fact that your mind can so vividly create a scenario, images, sounds and feelings that you can either live inside or observe is very revealing of your own mind, but *only* your mind. When relating a dream, we focus on the strangeness, on how odd everything looked, we never describe the sheer, marrow-deep terror the ghostly woman walking around your bed caused. Or the heart-racing, tear-inducing excitement of running up to the person you adore in the dream and telling them about how passionately you desire them. The emotions of a dream are like a soup you are submerged in. Dreams are made of how you feel not what happened, yet once we are out of them we subject them to the cold, rigid structure of a narrative that robs them of their weight and the flavour of significance they added to your day. The emotion in a book or film is carefully orchestrated and integrated into the characters and the storyline so it can have an emotional impact on the audience via a more objective medium. It even uses tools, such as foreshadowing, that come out of dream narratives to help with the association. There're whole theses written on how the language of cinema relates to how we dream but for now it is safe to say that narrative creation is integral to the relating of both.

The discussion of dreams ultimately boils down to their subjectivity, because a dream after all is pure subjectivity. The images and emotions that happen in your head can't be perfectly translated via an objective medium because you cannot impart your entire life experience and the nuance inherent in the way you feel about a given image or person. Trying to codify the abstract in a concrete way is at the heart of existence and we have developed narrative to do that. Be that in the way we observe events or the way we explain the innerworkings of our minds, humans have developed a method of translating reality into a communicable format that we call 'story'. By that I do not simply mean *all* interrelation is sequential to us, be that aural, physical or visual. Inside our heads, or zoomed out beyond our universe, or zoomed into a depth beyond the particles that are the fabric of existence, lies the purely abstract, and consequently *unstructured*, realm that we might refer to as, what Lacan called, 'The Imaginary'. Which is where the lily and the whale come in.

The image of the whale bursting from the lily is nonsensical but we can at least say it was present in my dream. The temptation is to try and explain it, despite the fact that the presence of the image means nothing to anyone except me and even then, it doesn't mean anything to me either. What it is, is a symbol which relates to the second of Lacan's 'Three Layers', the 'Symbolic', a layer of signs and signifiers which is where language occurs. Symbols communicate between the top layer, the 'Real', and the bottom layer, the 'Imaginary', and there is no doubt that a whale bursting from a flower is some sort of symbol. It is easy to say that image means nothing, it must be nonsense created by my subconscious mind (which it most certainly is) but the image of the flower and the image of the whale do represent something: a flower and a whale. The images mean something in the Imaginary but the only way they mean anything to you as a reader is with the words i.e. the symbols, of flower and whale, and yet more specifically, a sperm whale and a lily. Throughout my life I have built up the narrative of what a whale is and looks like, specifically sperm whales, from documentaries, books like *Moby Dick*, photographs and so on, and the same with flowers and lilies specifically. From past to present I have accrued meaning from these images and titles to form the symbols of a sperm whale and a lily flower. This Lacanian insight is a further example of why the illusion of sequential time is so integral to us and how closely story is related to that. What has happened with the lily and the whale is that *we have ascribed the images their meanings based on the narrative we created around them*. And, as a result, we extrapolate further meaning from there.

In broad terms: words have definitions, context gives them meaning. The image is a symbol, the narrative gives it value. This gives us the insight we need to understand that, first: we create narrative, and second: narrative is how we perceive reality. Through the abstract nature of dreams and the abstract science behind spacetime we are better able to understand how a narrative is essential to maintaining a form of cohesion in our lives and makes communication and interaction with other people and the real world possible. This may seem like a wildly grandiose claim but in the next chapter I'd like to try and explain how it is our perception of time that creates meaning and how this meaning is translated into narrative.

Chapter 3

Time's Eye

To understand why perception is so important to time – and therefore narrative – imagine time like a lens, either in your eye or in a camera. Like that lens, time can shift in and out of focus depending on the distance. This is also how we view certain events within a given timeline, or if you wanted to go all in on this idea of narrativisation: a storyline. Whatever event that happens we deem significant, in a quite literal sense, we focus on i.e. we give it meaning. Events that don't serve our overall narrative get pushed to the background and are therefore out of focus. It's a simple analogy but one that bears out, even when it comes to something like lens distortion.

Photographers might know how lenses that attempt to capture a particularly wide field of view onto an incompatibly small medium, such as a panoramic vista onto a 35mm rectangle of film, have a very deep curve to them that is visible on the image. This is known as 'lens distortion' and can manifest in certain ways, such as fringing, vignetting or curvature. In a rather beautiful parallel to this effect, high gravity, typically produced by dense orbs like planets or black holes, distorts spacetime too, which – as Einstein observed – would result in an observer of someone or something in a field of high gravity or moving at high speed, appearing to freeze, rendering them in sharp focus. This is often what people recall as happening in moments of high stress or trauma, reflecting that 'time slowed down'. These moments in cinema are even rendered using the camera technique of 'slow-motion'. So, an event that is given a huge level of *meaning* is given a great deal of *focus* and thus time is perceived to slow down.

What arises from these examples is that perception very much controls the flow of time, as does our concentration. I once heard relativity described as 'when you're in a dentist chair, a minute feels like an hour; when you're outside kicking a ball around an hour feels like a minute'. This is similar to the way we feel time 'skip' between sleeping and waking. We know that time has passed but we don't know how much, and it feels like we only just nodded off. That focus, or lack thereof, that we afford certain moments is further proof of how time is not the fixed process it is represented as. Of course, we are aware of these changes and differences to time as we perceive it and it would be foolish to start living your life believing that time can move backwards or that everything is relative (an idea we will explore further in the next part of the book) but what this understanding of time does do is show us that a shift in perspective can change almost everything about our world. This helps us better understand how we write our own stories and how we tell them to each other.

Narrative structure in fiction is reflected in our life stories. If we focussed on every single second of a single day in every single book, we'd end up with every book being *Ulysses*. As great a work of art as that novel may be, you would be unable to write and read a similar book every single day of your life. For that reason, we dispose of unessential information, only keeping the most important parts. What are the 'important parts' then? The lens analogy, again, is useful here. When looking at a dense view, like a forest or city skyline, the closer we are to it the less able we are to appreciate its size or significance. The phrase 'can't see the woods for the trees' is used for just this idea. But as we move further away from the woods or the skyline, we are better able to appreciate the scale of where we just were and, significantly, the elements of the forest that stand out the most, like the tallest trees, the hills and valleys you walked through earlier, and so on. This type of parallax, where distant objects not only reveal their prominence but also remain visible in the background, is an important factor in photography. Selecting the right lens to either allow the objects to appear closer together (a zoom lens) or keep their distance from each other (a wide-angle lens) gives you vastly different effects in the captured image. And in case you hadn't guessed, the same can be done with perspective through time. Events in a story that loom large in a character's history are clearly the significant ones, just like in real life. People and places become giants in our timeline when, at the time, they may not have seemed all that important. As Cervantes observed: 'Time ripens all things'.

To take the relation between time and vision even further, we use the word 'dilation' to describe the effect of our irises widening to let in more light so we are better able to see, also known as 'mydriasis', but the word is also used to describe the warping effect gravity has on spacetime. Dilation is originally a term used in morphology (with a mathematical description far beyond my understanding) that describes the widening of the area of an object. Dilation of the human iris is mimicked in photography by the aperture of a lens that, when fully open or 'stopped down', lets in the most amount of light but has the narrowest field of view. When the aperture is at its narrowest it lets in very little light but has the longest field of view. Yet again, we can use this same method of explaining our perspective of time and time itself. At the smallest, detail-orientated level, we see everything, it can overwhelm, but it is only when we open out our view that certain things or events come into sharp focus. It is no coincidence then that the lens for shooting objects very close up is called a 'macro' and not 'micro'.

By witnessing entropy through our eyes, we are creating time. *Time requires a lens to exist.* As ocularcentric as this view of existence is, it is undoubtedly the way we have evolved to best perceive reality. Time is almost entirely described in visual or ocular terms, so it makes sense that the inconsistencies we find in visual mediums translate too. While it is, of course, sensible to maintain a consistent experience of time day to day – being late for lunch can't be argued away by saying, 'I'm operating in a different temporal position to you,' trust me – it is important to be aware of how we all relate to time and how that influences our interactions. Entropy is, undeniably, a very real element in the universe that dictates our experience of it. However, how we relate to those experiences, what order they are put in and their significance to us is entirely of our own creation. For example, let's go back to those crystal champagne flutes.

As we discussed in the first chapter of this section, the events that resulted in the shattering of that single glass while another remained undisturbed on the table are difficult to place in a definitive temporal order. The state of entropy around those champagne glasses accelerates and decelerates, increases and decreases. It is only with an observer present we knew they were glasses at all, let alone what order the silica was melted down, reshaped and then shattered in. Thus, we, through the lens of our eyes, have created a narrative that strings these events together in a specific order that we call time. But there is something we are missing about the observation of the entropy infused champagne glasses.

Why?

Why did I select champagne glasses to represent entropy and the passage of time? Why did I throw the glass to the ground? Was I angry? Why was I angry? Why did I break one but leave the other untouched? Why did that other glass stay where it was in a house that was abandoned for years and eventually crumbled around it? Why was it me in the mini-narrative? Why were they crystal champagne flutes? Why not a painting that fell from the wall?

If I had not framed the shattering of the glass as merely an example and you were watching a film or TV show or looking at a painting or listening to your friend tell you about it, a lot of those questions might occur to you. Simply put, you would be looking for the *real* meaning behind the broken champagne flutes and, without realising you are doing it, you would start creating a narrative. A story would spring up around the events of the shattered champagne glass. Perhaps I was wearing a mourning suit? Maybe it was my wedding? Or just after? I threw the glass in disgust. Yes, there had been some dramatic falling out. No! My partner I had just married had been KILLED and, furious, cheated of my future with them, I hurled the glass to the floor, leaving my lover's glass untouched, awaiting lips to drink from it that will never come. Then I stormed out of our newly purchased house, still being built, never to return, haunted by the memories of my beloved, allowing it to fall to rack and ruin around the solitary champagne flute. A totem of tragedy that the unstoppable progress of time would eventually swallow. Or maybe *I* suffered a heart attack! I collapsed in a fit, causing the glass to hurtle across the room and shatter, sending it –

And so on. The sequence of events fast becomes insignificant to their reason or purpose. This is what we tend to think of when we talk about narrative: the story. The purpose of this section was to show that even something we believe to be as rigid and scientifically immutable as time is just as much a product of our subjective experience as everything else. In many ways, time is the base layer of narrative for the way we tell our bigger, broader stories. That is the Lie of Time, that it is simply part of the fabric of the universe and cannot be disputed. Time, and all its effects, is just as much a product of human invention as it is a product of entropy. In the next part we will look at how we construct these broader narratives and what they mean, now we have a better understanding of the abstract nature of entropy and our sequencing of events.

Part 3

Events

Chapter 1

Event Management

By framing time in this way, as a kind of 'subjective engine' that we have built around entropy to drive narrative, it begs the question, what are these narratives? And what do they mean? The most succinct way of describing how sequential time effects the meaning of our narratives is from Soren Kierkegaard, who observed in one of his diaries: 'Life can only be understood backwards; but must be lived forwards.' While seemingly obvious, like a lot of Kierkegaard's statements, it is singularly profound in that we live life through increasing levels of entropy, unaware of its results, but then apply logic to it retroactively. This form of 'backwards awareness' is what we are calling narrative. We will be looking at the 'lived forwards' part of Kierkegaard's phrase in another chapter, but as he is a thinker who is credited as one of the earliest existentialists, this idea he presents sends us head first into the question of free will.

How we progress through time/life/our narrative is key to the discussion of narrative because we apply meaning to moments past and moments present but does that then imply there is agency to the narrative going forward or is the agency only perceived in retrospect? I won't pretend to be able to solve the conundrum of free will and determinism here, but given modern research on the subject, there are some assumptions we can make. If modern research is to be believed – and it increasingly is – we live in a determinist universe. According to Newton's Third Law, 'For every action there is an equal and opposite reaction' and increasing studies into the area of causality are further cementing the idea that, though we are unable to conceive it, there is, on a microscopic level, a predetermined, logical and exact sequence of events from the Big Bang to the eventual heat death of the universe. Benjamin Libet's study of 'Readiness Potential' in the 1980s, where subjects were told to look at a clock and then at a time of their own choosing flick their wrist, measured the electrical impulses in the subject's brain to perform the task and compared it to the time the subjects gave when they did. The Readiness Potential (the brain activity that signals preparation to act) preceded the reported decision by half a second. For many, this unconscious preparation for an act was enough to convince them that determinism was a fact. Many studies since have borne out similar results. As such, this mode of thinking implies our identity, our decisions, our very being is merely electrical impulses produced by a thermodynamic engine degrading into a high state of entropy. This feeds into the bleaker ends of nihilistic philosophy that we see becoming increasingly more popular today, where people and characters live aimless, meaningless, empty lives and search for some form of fulfilment in this shallow existence. In short, this is a world without narrative.

While I believe this objective understanding of life to be (mostly) true, I don't think it really helps us. Let's take a recent study from 2002 into the effects of deterministic thinking by the psychologists Kathleen Vohs and Jonathan Schooler. In their study they told one group to read a document about free will being an illusion and then subjected them and a control group who had not read the document to a series of temptations. The result was that the group led to believe in a deterministic outcome of events, when offered the opportunity to cheat, did so; then when offered an opportunity to steal, did so. Those that had not read the paper did not cheat or steal. Further studies by Roy Baumeister of Florida State University have found that people led to believe free will is a lie are less likely to volunteer, lend their belongings or even give money to the homeless. Meaning that, while life does seem to be deterministic in nature, it is better – at least until we are better able to reconcile determinism's psychological effects – to live as if we have free will.

Another effect of determinism is one that, as far as I have researched, isn't really discussed as much and that is its theological component. On the face of it, determinism is a devoutly secular belief, Schoepenhauer's quote 'Man can do what he wills, but he cannot will what he wills' was often used by Einstein as a method of refuting free will, to 'free ourselves from this prison' of consciousness, as he put it. The problem with defining it as 'determinism' though, is that it suggests it has been 'determined' i.e. whether it be the ineffable, mathematical forces of the universe, or a benevolent, conscious being in the clouds, *something* has determined the outcome. As such, it seems somewhat contradictory for the scientific, atheistic or nihilistic, who denounce a higher power, to agree that a greater force controls them. You could almost say causality wove a narrative for us, like those sisters at the loom. This is not to say I am arguing for theism (let alone monotheism) but nor does it mean I am arguing for atheism either. Determinism is still the same, 'giving yourself up' to a higher power inherent in any religious doctrine but it is, perplexingly, never seen this way. Given its association with objective reason and the scientific method, determinism does seem to be the way of the universe, but, like all narratives, it is not the only one. As we discussed in Part 1, for a narrative to be 'true' (not 'real') it must be consistent and there must be consensus. Both determinism and free will as narratives for human experience lack firm consistency and consensus. While that may change with future research, given what we are experiencing in the contemporary moment, it may be better to understand how both narratives may be seen to operate at the same time.

Take the random, chaotic adventures depicted in *Bojack Horseman, Rick and Morty* and *True Detective*, that seem to capture a certain nihilistic zeitgeist about learning to cope with the lack of control in modern society and the meaninglessness of life in the developed world today. This relates to what the philosopher Albert Camus called the Absurd. For Camus the Absurd was best summed up by Sisyphus who was cursed to roll a rock up and down that mountain for eternity. Camus related that to every day existence and how pointless our lives are in a universe that consistently rejects meaning. His solution to this, as he put it in the memorable final line of his essay *The Myth of Sisyphus*, is to 'imagine Sisyphus happy'. By this he meant Sisyphus should be thought of as projecting meaning onto his task, in the same way we imbue meaning into our daily tasks. For our purposes, we can call this narrativisation.

How we 'read' our narrative is just as important as how we produce it. Whether we are active participants in choosing its path or purely reactionary in organising what is given to us, we are still imposing meaning on our decisions, still creating a narrative. We are constantly, in effect, *managing the events of our lives*. This is not said to dismiss the discussion of determinism and free will but is an attempt to better make use of events as we experience them. The idea of time travel is one that persists in fiction and (to some degree) in science today but instead of asking if we could do it and what would happen if we did have it, a more salient question might be, *why* would we do it? The interactions of particles, between thermodynamic engines, moving through the process of entropy would dictate returning or reassigning all these elements to their previous states, which sounds almost feasible when looked at from an objective, scientific point of view but the whole reason we want to travel through time is because of events we have given meaning in the past and because we want to see events that may contain meaning in the future. As well as all the paradoxes inherent in time travel the one that fiction doesn't often explore is the fact that it relies on being able to look back and reflect on past events and their meanings. We are not simply asking to change the interactions of different elements, we seek to alter their meaning. When we talk about time travel, we are, in fact, talking about altering narrative, which means by extension, in an abstract way time travel is totally possible. Sights, smells and sounds are all profound triggers for memory and can give you the feeling, the metaphorical 'Proustian Rush', of being back in the past as we remember it. I also know plenty of people who have altered narratives of their past to better suit their present. All of this, however, is dependent on how we 'understand backwards', how we have 'read' history.

The important factor to take away from 'understanding backwards and living forwards' is that they are both concordant with our temporal position (the present) regardless of input or output. Both free will and determinism are restrictive, unhelpful and even detrimental to our daily lives if subscribed to wholly. Narrative, on the other hand, has utility in day to day life, allowing, as it does, the ability (or at least appearance of our ability) to control the in-flow and out-flow of events. To better clarify this, admittedly abstract, idea, I am going to use an example from one of the most popular narratives of modern times, and for that, I can only apologise.

In *Harry Potter and the Half-Blood Prince,* protagonist and student Potter is arguing with Jungian 'Guide' and Headmaster Dumbledore over a prophecy that says Potter must be the one to kill Voldemort. While I am aware using Harry Potter as an avatar for any kind of debate is considered problematic at best and utterly insipid at worst, I posit that this dialogue at the end of chapter 23 perfectly illustrates the necessity of meaning – provided by narrative – to create perspective on these kinds of existential discussions. Dumbledore and Harry are essentially debating determinism with Harry arguing that this prophecy has essentially made his decision – the decision to fight Voldemort to the death – for him. When Harry points this out, in frustration, Dumbledore snaps back: 'You are setting too much store by the prophecy! ... The prophecy does not mean you *have* to do anything!' The wise old wizard is essentially pointing out that with or without the deterministic value of a prophecy Potter would fight his nemesis to the death anyway. While events may have been set in motion outside of Harry's control, it is the *meaning in those events that makes the discussion of agency irrelevant.* It is 'the difference between being dragged into the arena to face a battle to the death and walking into the arena with your head held high'. Far from being a deterministic, empty, nihilistic existence without meaning, nor being a God-given paradise of free will, by creating a narrative around entropy and its effects, both can be seen to operate at the same time. The circumstance is predetermined but free will impacts its meaning. The narrative is more important than the decision itself. In short, by understanding it backwards, we can live it forwards.

Discussions of being and time can go on for days but suffice to say I am not trying to formulate a decisive understanding of existence, merely exploring how we already interpret it. The trouble with arguing that we do have control over events means we come up against the very issues we face in society today, that controlling narratives has troubling ramifications on their meaning. This is because whoever considers themselves author of that narrative imposes their meaning on it, which as we said earlier is why the context of presenting a story must be handled with care. It is less of a problem if it is your individual narrative, but more of a problem if it is a broader societal narrative such as race or gender. We will be looking closely at these broader narratives in the final part of this book but in the next chapter we will explore this idea of imbuing the moment with meaning and how narrative creation arises from that.

Chapter 2

The Main Event

So far, we have been looking at broader understandings of narratives, their contexts and their drives, but while this serves as a useful meta-commentary on life, how does this apply to moment-to-moment existence? We only ever perceive existence in the present moment, which modern neuroscience has declared as being a period of around 3 to 4 seconds. That's a lot of moments every day, and a lot of meaningless moments at that. But what about the ones that aren't, the ones that are significant? Life changing, even? It is easy to see how these fit easily into a narrative. The death of a loved one, the loss of a job, the meeting of a partner, all of these events mean something as they happen but come to mean different things over time. In the same way you will re-read or re-watch a story with a surprise ending that then allows the story to develop a new narrative consistency, you will go back over previous events with a fresh consensus on what happened, thus giving it new meaning. This is useful for these bigger, 'life changing' moments but where we see narrative operating most overtly is in coincidence.

This chapter is why I wanted to write this book. Despite being secular, I have always believed 'things happen for a reason' due to various experiences throughout my life that have seemed far too opportune, well-timed and, yes, consistent to be without reason. But if I don't believe in any entity arranging or performing these events just for little old me, then why am I so sure there is reason behind these various confluences of events? I found my answer, or at least the beginnings of one, when I read about Carl Jung's concept of 'synchronicity' that argues events are not only linked by causality but by meaning.

A brief note on Carl Jung: he is a difficult one. He falls into that modern category of 'problematic fave' for me. As someone who flirted with fascism and whose thinking is adopted by some deeply troubling individuals today, I understand distance should be kept. Unfortunately, he is one of the few theorists who took an interest in developing inherently subjective ideas like the soul and dreams, so that they might be better interpreted and their significance in objective reality be better observed. His work on symbols is also hugely successful for a reason, theories borne out by modern psychoanalysis that reveals the importance of symbolism in catharsis. As such, his theories are quite useful in the context of this book, but I am aware of the difficulties in separating out some of the less than savoury aspects of his ideas from those with actual worth. Needless to say, take my referencing with a pinch of salt, but a better understanding of some of his concepts is, I feel, warranted today given his resurgence in popularity.

My discovery of the theory of synchronicity led me to further research with a constant eye on where our concept of meaning comes from. Some years later when the discussion of narrative became more and more commonplace in the media, I started to understand the connection. Or rather, I began to develop my own narrative about it. Our perception of time, our need to create meaning, the in-built tendency to develop narratives, these all seemed to be best explained in three linked but distinct concepts that revolve around meaning and the moment: synchronicity, coincidence and luck.

To define terms, luck is an event without meaning in the cause or causal object, but we add meaning to its result. For example: you drop your keys as a loose slate topples from a roof, you turn and collect the keys only to hear the slate shatter behind you where you were standing moments before. With relief you say, 'phew! That was lucky!' to yourself. The dropping of the slate was an accident, entropy at work, nothing anyone did caused it or could predict it, but it would most certainly have killed you if you had not stopped because, again, by another pure matter of entropy, you dropped your keys. What luck!

Coincidence is an event where the causes or causal objects have no apparent connection but are seen to have purpose in their result. For example, the world-famous electric guitarist and songwriter Jimi Hendrix lived at 23 Brook Street, right next door to the former home of celebrated eighteenth-century composer George Handel at number 25. Hendrix did not know this when renting the place and Handel certainly didn't. What a coincidence!

Synchronicity is similar to coincidence, but Jung posited that the causes or causal objects that led to a remarkable or unlikely event were linked by meaning. The result is the perception of the event as having some element of reason to it. An example from my own life:

I wanted to buy a specific model guitar in a specific colour. I'm left-handed so perfect guitars don't just turn up, you have to order them. I was finally in a position to buy the instrument so that day, on my lunch break, I left work, went to my local music shop and went up to one of the assistants. The encounter went something like this:

'Hello, I was wondering if I could order a specific guitar?'

Not looking up from a piece of paper he was writing on, the assistant said, 'Yeah we can do that. What are you after?'

'I'm after a left-handed, Mexican made, Fender Telecaster, preferably in red. Please.'

Without looking up, the man said, 'like that one behind you in the window, you mean?'

I turned and there it was, the exact guitar I wanted. I hadn't seen it in the window as I passed, it had only come in the day before and was second hand, making it considerably cheaper than RRP. Not only all that, I happened to have enough cash in my pocket for a deposit. For the next 2 days I told everyone this story, exclaiming at the end '*It was meant to be!*' I believed it had happened for a reason.

Statistically this and all the examples above are bound to happen sooner or later but given the circumstances, like how long I lusted after that specific guitar, its typical difficulty in acquiring, the timing of its return to the store, its lower price when I frankly shouldn't have been spending the money, this all seemed too perfect a confluence of events not to be driven by reason. That guitar was *mine*, by fate or by fiction.

This sort of thing is occasionally called a 'Movie Moment', in that it makes logical sense for these events to converge and can easily be seen to fit in the narrative of a fiction. Without our conscious minds present to observe these happenings they have no reason or meaning at all, these are just interactions of molecules and particles, but our minds are present, and we bring our narratives to these interactions. Given that we have explored how we create narratives retroactively, these examples show how we carry these narratives with us in the moment so that, as they happen, events can be made to have logical sense to them. This logic is our own in that we have imbued the objects with meaning, so that as these objects move together or apart in our temporal plane, we create the narrative to justify it. In short, it happens for a reason. A reason we invented.

It is worth contrasting coincidence and synchronicity, events that we narrativise and thus project notions of meaning onto, with events that we think lack reason or logic. Luck and chance are different methods of describing events that aren't consistent with a narrative we are creating. Luck is the least convincing excuse for an event as it relieves us of any agency and gives it to a type of amorphous, poorly-defined-yet-somehow-benevolent-and-altruistic 'energy', occasionally even personifying it as a 'Lady'. Not only is it a lazy method of explaining a random encounter, it's a lazy method of narrative. There's a reason one of Pixar's '22 Rules for Storytelling' is 'Coincidences to get characters into trouble are great; coincidences to get them out of it are cheating.' Luck is a cheat for getting you out of trouble.

Chance, on the other hand, is just another way of referring to entropy. It is appropriate for when we feel we have no agency but don't wish to personify the causal process. Chance has no intent, it is neither good nor bad. Chance, like entropy, simply says 'anything can happen'. If we look at people who actively try to control narratives, unforeseen events are often placed at the altar of good or bad luck. That is, if they even acknowledge that events were out of their – or someone's – hands at all. It is better for the narrative if it is somebody's fault or success.

Fortune is not dissimilar but important to note due to the fact that fortune is a form of narrative itself. It equally accounts for a certain lack of agency on the individual's behalf but tends to be seen as operating *with* someone's choices to facilitate their success. 'Fortune favours the bold' as the saying goes. Declaring your wealth 'my fortune' too implies it was a *series* of fortunate events that led you to be in its possession. You can be fortunate, in the same way you can be 'lucky' (Fortuna being the Roman goddess of luck) but if you say you gained something by being lucky it is seen as an unearned gift, if you are fortunate you at least worked for it.

As I said before, the topic of this chapter is what made me want to write about narrativisation because whether discussing luck, chance, fortune, coincidence or synchronicity they are all *a method for creating meaning out of random, entropic interactions*. We use logic to define events, that imbues them with meaning, which then offers us a reason. Which – for me at least – reconciles my secular beliefs in an objective universe with my certainty that 'everything happens for a reason'. Events happen for a reason because we tell them to.

We have looked at 'understanding backwards' and reasoning the moment, but what of looking ahead and projecting narratives into the future as so many of us do? The explanation leads us to discuss the 'lived forwards' portion of Kierkegaard's observation from earlier in this section and why this is probably the most important part of narrativisation.

Chapter 3

Eventually

If narrativisation can only be accomplished in the moment by 'understanding backwards' that doesn't stop us from trying to second guess entropy's designs by projecting narratives into the future. Whether it's statistical or data models that look ahead (methods which are essential to the sciences and economics) or whether it's more simplistic pattern recognition projections like 'today is Wednesday which means tomorrow it will be Thursday', we are constantly looking ahead. Going back to Part 2's discussion of space and time, unlike travelling through a physical space where you know where you've been, where you are and can see where you are going, travelling through time is less easy to navigate. The biggest difference between the two is compulsion. Moving through space is typically voluntary, moving through time is not. The other major difference is that temporal spaces other than the one we are in are far more difficult to perceive. While evidence and memory aggregate to an understanding of the past we are not allowed to 'travel back' to a past moment to recollect it in the same way we can in a physical space. Looking ahead is just as difficult, we can predict based on certain methods what will happen in the near future but even that is not a guarantee, just ask any gambler. You cannot see ahead of you in the same way you can in a physical space. What is confusing about these distinctions is that if we define spacetime as one and the same thing, why can we see through space and not time? The answer is that space is part of objective reality, whereas time is subjective. This answer helps give us a clearer view of narrativisation and, significantly, its dangers.

Predicting the future tends to be seen as risible fodder for sci-fi and fantasy stories, frauds with crystal balls and astrologers, and yet we still defer to politicians, businesses, 'trend-setters', 'taste-makers', market forces, news anchors, columnists, credit scores and more every day. Our daily existence is planned weeks, months and years ahead by ourselves and others. But, as discussed earlier regarding the past, for this to function as an accurate or helpful narrative, it needs consistency and consensus. In the same way as our personal and global history is a subjective entity, so is the future, and just like the past, the future can be written by a victor. Those who control the narrative now are better able to write the future purely through narrative design. Many world leaders in our contemporary moment, with consensus for their narrative of the past, are currently discussing how their narrative for the future is for the best. As we explored earlier, their past narrative may be a fiction but by accruing support the narrative gathers consensus even where it lacks consistency, this then leads to support for completely unfounded predictions and plans for the future, simply because they have a controlling stake in the present. In this way we can see the further power of narrative. And this doesn't just apply to global politics but personal narratives. Failure is transient, it would be impossible to fail at everything, all the time, every day, but if failure has been prominent to your recent past or your present, we quickly project this narrative of failure into the future. A narrative that, with a shockingly high suicide rate in the UK and the USA, can sometimes lead to devastating consequences.

We have names for this method of future narrativisation, like prophecy, or portent or augur, all of which tend to have a history in antiquity when characters like Cassandra who was 'cursed' by the ability to see the future but unable to have her predictions believed. While there is a great truth to this, both in how painful truths and predictions are dismissed even today and the way in which women's narratives are ignored (especially when being honest and making accurate predictions), the overarching tone when referring to *this* type of narrative projection is that of magic or mysticism i.e. it is dismissed. Power does not accept narratives of the past or future except from itself. We see the dangers of this today specifically when it comes to climate change, where there is an absolute consistency of evidence and a majority consensus among the scientific community, but the narrative is disputed in favour of a preferred narrative that is subjectively more appealing to a wealthy and powerful few. It is notable that the most avid climate change deniers live in areas where climate change is less obvious in its effects and are typically wealthy people who would only stand to lose out in business were better measures to combat climate change put into effect. Essentially, one narrative is clashing with another. When it comes to the past, however, this feels less urgent. Disputes over historical narratives, while important, are less cataclysmic than disputes over our very ability to survive the future and it's here we touch upon the purpose of this book.

As we will look at in greater depth in the fifth and final part, narrative performs multiple functions: it is our way of organising reality so that it is comprehensible to us, it is a way of contextualising ourselves in society, it is a way of relating to others, it is how we construct identity, it is a mode of catharsis, it is a method of enjoyment and so much more. This does not mean however, that narrative is a purely post-modern, abstract, subjective thing that has no effect on the real world; on the contrary, it is profoundly important to the real world. The idea that a narrative rooted in climate science is not essential to how we continue as a species – a very objective, reality-based process – is absurd. Narrative is a way of relating our subjective existence with our objective one that is dictated by our perception of time. Our survival is a subjective concern, global climate an objective one. The attempt to reconcile these two elements *for our own good* requires a narrative to be created. The issue we have stumbled upon in the age of the internet, social media and the 24-hour news cycle is that there are lots of contrasting narratives that therefore clash. This is not simply a question of 'History being Written by the Victors'; how we see the future is utterly reliant on who does the writing too.

Discussions of free will and determinism play strongly into this because, while we may lean more towards one definition of existence or the other, we are still 'living forwards' and the practical aspects of living life usurp the need for immediate answers on broader existential concerns. Narrative provides a working solution to the problem that allows either to be true, and even if one were to be conclusively proved (and, as stated, determinism seems more and more to be the likely winner) that still has little effect on our narratives. If it's all free will that guides our existence, we are already deciding our future with narrative, but if it's all predetermined, we still have to utilise narrative to 'enter the arena with our head held high' or risk being dragged through time without any consideration for the future at all.

To tell a story about the future can be as simple as saying 'The bus will be here in five minutes', to being as complicated as something like Hegel's dialectics, but however we do it, we have to do it. The necessity of looking where you are going and where you have been is essential in travelling through space, just as it is in travelling through time. In the same way we built the roads, paths and towns we travel along to reach our destination, so have we written the narratives we travel through into the future. This makes the need for strong, consistent and consensus driven narratives utterly essential for 'living forwards', because, like it or not, we *are* living forwards and we currently lack any consensus or consistency in our future.

While the last two parts have been concerned with more abstract ideas of narrative, in the next section I will attempt to solidify the three main elements of narrative we all know as a method of developing a working usage of it for everyday life.

Part 4

Narrative

me, however, that it shares its definition with the literal sense of getting people 'on board' a vessel. Once you are on board a ship it is hard to disembark, not without risk at any rate. This style of beginning is indicative of the corporate world and how their narrative use is not only dehumanising but clearly influenced by the language of the military and all that implies. Sun Tzu's *The Art of War* is still sold in the business section of major bookshops after all. It is an attempt to make the idea of starting or beginning seem more objective and mechanical, like a lot of business speak, but instead it comes loaded with more context than its users would probably like. As usual, it is an attempt to remove the humanity and the emotion from something to make it seem more objective and irrefutable that only serves to point out how subjective it is, and beginnings are no exception. What the corporate understanding of beginnings shows us, however, is an aspect of starting narrative that often gets overlooked.

When advertising to people and attempting to onboard customers, businesses will do their best to obtain as much demographic information as possible. We have seen in recent years how rampant and unethical this data gathering has become thanks to well publicised leaks regarding the practices of Cambridge Analytica and Facebook, but those wishing to use this data know how essential it is to the onboarding process. To start a narrative, we must obtain all the information we possibly can about the story. This is a process we will call 'gathering'. The mode of gathering is different depending on the narrative you want to tell: corporations gather consumer information to start their product story, start-up businesses gather market information to understand how to start their business, writers gather research into their chosen topic, we gather knowledge around our birth to know where we started. It is only with all this information that we are able to start anything. If we deem a given event of our choosing 'the beginning' then this gathering is what comes before that. Narratives do not start in a vacuum and this is the method by which we are able to ascertain a more solid foundation for the beginning of our stories.

But if beginnings are so subjective, is 'beginning' the right word to use? A better way of describing it might be to refer to them as 'openings'. If you think of when a shop opens, it only opens when the staff have arrived, the tills are prepared, the shelves are stocked; it only opens when it is ready to open. A public official doesn't 'declare this new library: Open!' when it is still a pile of rubble and brick, the moment that would be described as the building's 'beginning', it opens – somewhat counterintuitively – when it is 'finished'. The idea of an opening instead of a beginning implies it is contingent on other narratives being complete before it can start. Openings can be moved too. Opening times for public buildings fluctuate throughout the year, 'finding an opening' in a job market or sports match shifts significantly. 'Being open' also implies a willingness for analysis that can change at any time too. A story is only offered, it only starts, when the person writing or telling it is ready for it to be seen and critiqued by others. The cinema industry often refers to the release of a film as its 'opening', and a strong or weak 'opening weekend' can ultimately determine the film's future. Openings are a subjective start point that react to other narratives and define what follows. A beginning is seen as an objective start point, the moment of parthenogenesis that begins the developmental cycle of a narrative. Both are flawed descriptors, but each serves a different type of story you might want to tell.

While beginnings are so dependent on the ending of other narratives, gathering information prior to the event and, mainly, our own preference for the most resonant start point, they rely just as heavily on the rest of the story. Where to start that story of the Vietnam War is contingent on the tale you want to tell about it. *Apocalypse Now* tells an affecting tale of the madness of war and the pointlessness of the conflict by 'coming in late', whereas *Full Metal Jacket* tells just as affective a tale with those themes but focusses more on the effects upon the American soldiers than the nation and populace of Vietnam by starting months before their deployment. Another Kubrick film, *2001: A Space Odyssey,* starts at the dawn of man and ends in the space age. These beginnings are as equally dependent on their endings as they are on the histories gathered before it. The sections of the narrative you are telling are interlinked and totally dependent on one another. We will be developing that idea in the next chapter.

Chapter 2

Middles

It is surprisingly difficult to define a 'middle' as it occurs in stories because this is generally what we consider the narrative itself. To discuss a middle is to talk about the most substantial part of the narrative and without reference to a specific example, that is quite difficult. Also, having explained why I'm no fan of the hermeneutic method of deconstructing narrative given by Campbell, it feels redundant to then attempt to define narrative structure in the same singular, prescriptive way. But for that reason, we would end up just describing the middle of a story as 'The bit where all the stuff happens'. In an attempt to tread the fine line of not dismissing the variety and subjectivity inherent in creating narratives but also explaining its structure, perhaps the best way to define the bulk of a story's narrative is as 'change'.

The reason we tell a story is typically to explain in detail how we get from point A to point B and the narrative is the road that takes us there. The fundamental aspect of a story is that the elements presented at the opening are altered by its end. Change has occurred. Even in the shortest stories, an anecdote or flash fiction, say, we are explaining how the state of a champagne glass altered from whole to shattered. Were we to leave the room, the glass whole, then re-enter the room with the glass broken, we would want to know how, surely? We immediately create the beginning and the end of the narrative but are confused as to its transition. If this narrative is missing it becomes a mystery and is only solved when a narrative is introduced. A narrative, then, could be described as a 'mode of change'.

In Yeats' poem *The Second Coming,* believed to have been written in 1919, he says that 'Things fall apart; the centre cannot hold'; reflecting the tumult left after the First World War, but this phrase has recently been taken up on social media by multiple different groups referring to the 'political centre'. These 'centre' parties and groups have dominated mainstream politics for the last 30 years or more but given the polarisation of discourse today, the centre finds itself with increasingly less support. A quick search on Twitter reveals both those on the Left and Right reiterate Yeats' quote, while those who identify as 'Centrists' use it as a warning to maintain their heading, to hold their course. This reading of the poem with regard to a centre in politics is fascinating in its misinterpretations but also in its commitment to an idea of a 'centre' to politics at all. If we see politics as a narrative (which it is) but also as something that *uses* narrative, this 'Middle Way' (or 'Third Way' as British Prime Minister Tony Blair called it) is openly transitional by design, precisely what Yeats was referring to. By attempting to appease voters of both the Left and Right with conflicting policies, settling on neither a determined socialist strategy nor a wholly Conservative one, it can never remain dominant because there is nowhere for it to go. The centre *cannot* hold. This is also where the other misinterpretation of the poem, and not just regarding policy, comes in. The poem is called *The Second Coming* because Yeats is waiting for an imminent change: 'Surely some revelation is at hand.' The centre cannot hold because of this suspected transition. The narrative in the poem, the same as the cultural narrative the world was experiencing at the time, is that of change; perhaps it is so actively reproduced online today because it says that 'the best lack all conviction, while the worst \ Are full of passionate intensity.' For our purposes, Yeats' 'centre' perfectly describes this middle transition of narrative. A point we look on as even more prescient given that he was writing between two catastrophic conflicts, a period we often forget about, defining the generation growing up then as 'Lost', because we subconsciously link those two wars as if one era. Yeats could not have known what was coming but with his astute and remarkable gift of perception and fidelity in his writing he was able to see this transitional 'centre' for what it was and, perhaps unintentionally, predicted the conflict to come. A second coming indeed.

This central change is not just present in cultural narratives but artistic ones too. For instance, in pop music there is sometimes a section where the trajectory of a song changes briefly in the middle for eight bars, often referred to as the 'Middle 8' (this bar limit fluctuates considerably, it came out of mid-twentieth century pop music when the change had to be kept short for airplay reasons; that changed pretty quickly so it's not a hard and fast rule). The Middle 8 is still used today in pop song writing (occasionally substituted for the much-maligned instrumental) to add texture and variance to the song. It will often switch to major or minor tonality depending on what chords the rest of the song uses, sometimes it changes rhythm (the Beatles' 'We Can Work It Out' does both, switching from major in 4/4 to minor ¾ in the middle) but it is always an acknowledged change from the rest of the song as the constant repeat of verse and chorus can become boring after a couple of rounds.

In narrative fiction this change is sometimes called a 'twist'. These are sometimes put towards the end if the creator wants to draw attention to it and the purpose of the story is to make you aware of the change in a 'meta' way. The most common use of a twist in movies, TV and books, though, is in the middle. They are often subtle but significant twists that allow for change rather than enacting it. A good example of this is in the work of Wes Anderson whose entire filmography revolves around a shocking or violent moment in the centre of his stories (the suicide attempt in Tenenbaums, the helicopter crash in Zissou, the death of the boy in Darjeeling Ltd, etc) that prompts the characters into action and therefore change. For Campbell this was 'the abyss' or 'the revelation' that tested the hero most, but in more general terms it's an inciting act that allows for development of characters or plot.

This concept of a 'twist' to create change can even be seen in similarly explicit fashion in poetry. The 'volta' (Italian for 'turn') is used in classical poetic forms like the sonnet to signify a change in the perspective of the poem. Sonnets, for instance, typically have a turn somewhere after line eight. Shakespeare's twenty-ninth sonnet begins with the conditional clause 'When, in disgrace with Fortune and men's eyes,' and continues with it for the next nine lines until he finally releases the grammatic tension with 'Haply I think on thee'. The volta is often used in poetry as an opportunity for counterpoint, a change that offers an alternative point of view. A method shared in dialectical discourse that offers a thesis, antithesis and synthesis. If we consider the thesis and synthesis the beginning and end of a dialectic narrative then the antithesis is its middle, the centre where it changes.

Here seems appropriate to reassert my refutation of this explanation of narrative as an attempt at the same sort of hermeneutics that Freud, Jung, Marx, Campbell and the other Modernist thinkers were fans of, and we are seeing a resurgence in today. On the contrary, my attempt to define this structure is to reconcile this need for objective study with the subjective experience. Trying to take subjective concepts such as emotions or change and treat them to the kind of objective analysis provided by hermeneutics is, to coin a phrase, 'high cotton' for anyone wishing for something solid in a post-Modern age that treats everything as changeable and subjective. People who feel disenfranchised or abstracted from society where once they had a concrete interaction with it (be that through a job as a labourer, their hobby as a collector, their social interaction in bars and clubs), understandably will wish to return to that. But given that the internet doesn't seem to be going away and our perspective on the rest of the world is fundamentally altered because of that, a return to that more 'rustic' interaction with culture and society isn't coming back. On the other hand, this does not mean complete abstraction is the best method for progress, as we are discovering it's a pretty poor one, something I begrudgingly accept as a valid criticism by some of those voices whom I would not otherwise identify with. Instead this is an attempt at a form of synthesis that allows for analysis in a material, 'real world' sense, but does not deny the subjective nature of our experience. To return to the topic, change is a real, measurable and important element to life that can be objectively studied but the change only *means* something because of us. Narrative, it seems to me, is a good way of expressing this attempt at praxis.

The changes we're discussing serve to create narrative tension in fiction, but we could call it narrative 'pressure' for the real life narrativisation we see today. Without this pressure, without a middle, there is no story. It is usually released by the story's end and we are better able to appreciate the change wrought by the narrative. Given the current climate it could be argued we are currently experiencing high levels of this form of narrative pressure and finding that the centre really cannot hold. Because of this we are all hoping for a release of this tension, 'its hour come round at last', and doing our best to find a form of ending or conclusion which is what we shall explore in the next chapter.

Chapter 3

Endings

In the same way as narrativisation demands, 'where does a story start?' it also begs the question 'where does a story end?' And just like a beginning, it isn't in the place you think. The same rules apply to choosing where to end a narrative in that it is just as subjective as choosing where to start it. Using the same example as we did in the 'Beginning' section, if we are looking at your life as a narrative, death is not necessarily the 'End' either. For a lot of people, perspective on their life, their memories, their conscious agency and so on, will have deteriorated to a lesser or greater degree the more they age and the closer they get towards the end of their life. And while you – or your understanding of you, we might say – may end, that does not mean the narrative of you ends as well. Shakespeare's been dead for quite a while now but that doesn't stop a new story about him popping up every few years. Shakespeare's narrative not only continues, it is in rude health. This is not an attempt to dismiss death (or birth for that matter) as purely subjective, it is one of the single most important and affecting events in everyone's lives but understanding how a narrative end is perceived will always involve death. Of course, death is the most obvious but not the only representation of an end. A business will end, a meal will end, a fire will end, a day will end, anything can – and inevitably will – end. What constitutes an ending then?

Endings all have the property of finality. In this sense finality means that which is irreversible. This is the inevitable consequence of the 'middle' of a narrative that enacts change. Change (or entropy, as we discussed in Part 2) isn't reversible, so the resultant state is final. This 'essence of finality' then is what constitutes an ending, or at least gives us that sense of an ending. This, like all narrativisation, operates on a macro or micro scale. From the end of a champagne flute to the end of a large-scale conflict, the end does not occur until this finality is reached. Before that, things are changeable and in flux. The decision to throw the glass, or the various political successes and losses that lead to an end in conflict, for instance, are mutable. A small narrative, when combined, contributes to larger narratives so consequently larger narratives are made up of smaller ones. But unless finality is achieved, there is no story, which suggests the interesting idea *you cannot begin that story without the ending.*

Just as we said in the first chapter of this section, beginnings are contingent on the ending of another narrative, but this also extends to the narrative you are attempting to tell. To approach narrative in its state of change (i.e. the middle) is almost impossible as you don't know what the story is. The only way a true narrative is constructed is by 'understanding backwards', even when 'living forwards' our projections for the future are based on a conclusion that is reached, we do not simply say 'weather will change' when discussing climate science, we predict by how much and by when. It puts narrative in that contradictory position Kierkegaard gave us of being *a backwards process that can only be expressed forwards.* The essence of Time's Lie. This also puts a focus on the subjectivity of endings and reveals them as a method of processing. Endings are created by the meaning we have imbued in the preceding change, this being another example of our natural desire to create narratives. This also makes explicit something that feels self-evident but is regularly refuted: *endings are not natural occurrences.*

'Death is a part of life' is a phrase I have heard many, many times in my life. In addition to it being a glib philosophy on the transience of life, it also functions as a banal platitude offered to those grieving. Death, decay, change, these are all very much part of life and their influence on narrativisation is essential, but as mentioned, these are not necessarily 'final' parts of a narrative.

Death is not an ending that can be experienced and subsequently narrativised by the individual because…well…they're dead. Equally those still living are unable to contextualise death in the way we do with every other experience because we don't experience it. Death is certainly an ending as it is obviously quite final for the person it happens to, but they don't know that (this is assuming you are of the belief, like I am, that there is no life after death, of course). Endings, due to their finality, feel unnatural to us, which is why we respond to them in such extreme ways. We experience the end of things as a jarring moment, a break, that is only reconciled and understood after the fact.

In his book *Samuel Richardson and the Theory of Tragedy*, James Smith compares this 'break' to the technique of caesura commonly used in poetry, a caesura being a point, typically in the middle of a line, where one statement ends and another begins. Smith likens the event of Clarissa's rape by the rake Lovelace in Richardson's novel to this technique, as a fracture point for the narrative. It can be seen in the narrative of the novel as a point of change (it's in the middle of the book after all) but equally the point at which one narrative ends and another begins. Smith pursues this idea that the caesura is the point of tragedy because it is the point of trauma. The element of finality in Lovelace's rape of Clarissa is expressed in the broken, fragmentary prose after the rape takes place; this traumatic event ended one period and began another. This sense of ending is different to the narrative of the book as a whole, which charts the overarching story of Clarissa's life, but perfectly chimes with our understanding of change and finality, and the idea that larger narratives necessitate smaller narratives within. The idea of the caesura as a moment of trauma is a powerful one, though. These breaks, or endings, typically come unexpectedly, quite literally in the middle of the line, yet force a continuation, just as an ending *forces* us to construct a narrative due to its finality, which is equally an example of how unnatural endings are. The caesura relies on the expectancy of the completion of a line of poetry unimpeded, coming to a 'natural end'. An ending, however it occurs, is always preferably deferred, the finality resisted, until we are better prepared, never acknowledging the fact we will likely never be prepared for it. Our idealised belief in a good, right and 'natural' end is often at odds with the reality of how things end in a more objective sense. Someone dies, our priceless heirloom breaks, a secret is revealed, we are physically traumatised, all are unwelcome, all are endings, and, thanks to entropy, all are irreversible, thus the ending is traumatic because we do not understand it, having never experienced an ending 'from the inside', as it were. It is symbolic then that caesuras in poetry are often created by a full stop.

The need for a healthier understanding of narrative ending is still not given the attention it deserves. In a less theoretical sense, society's refusal to deal with ending is causing us existential problems. Our method of waste disposal is woefully under equipped for the twenty-first century, with plastics clogging the oceans and landfills overflowing. In his book *Ends*, Joe Macleod looks at our relationship with finality and how this impacts us materially by pointing out the disastrous effects of not managing the 'end of life' of products. He argues that as focussed on innovation and 'onboarding' (a phrase I learned from his book) as companies are, they should focus on the end of the product's lifespan at exactly the same time as its development begins, just as they should look at how best to help customers leave (or 'offboard') when they sign them up. A business that builds a method of finality into its model will function better and less harmfully when entropy comes around – as it always does – to bring things to a close. Macleod sites the ease with which customers can cancel and reinstate their Netflix account as one of the factors that makes them a high growth company with near impeccable customer satisfaction levels. Approaches to death with similar forethought are *always* preferable to the shock and unpreparedness that normally greets the passing of someone we love. As someone who was better able to prepare for the death of a loved one emotionally, the trauma of that event was so significantly reduced I look upon my family's time in the hospital with a sad fondness. Staying with mortality, even the better disposal of human remains is an environmental issue today and careful thought and discussion with someone before they die about how they wish their remains to be handled greatly reduces stress on the family and, if done right, is more environmentally friendly too. With these examples we can see how great an effect ending has, but we can equally see our need to recognise it at the beginning of our narratives, so it is not just seen as a moment to be reached. A way we can do this, like our 'gathering to open' for beginnings discussed earlier, is to 'disassemble to close'.

Like we gather elements to begin a story, or to 'open' it as we explored, we must disassemble those elements to finish. The change that has occurred to the different parts of the narrative must be taken apart at its close, so we might better come to that crucial understanding that narrative offers. We see this in the way we separate themes from fictional narratives as well as lived ones. The most obvious example in modern media is the 'post-mortem' of a movie that comes as soon as we are out of the screening room. On the drive home, or at the pub afterwards, we pore over the details of the narrative to better come to an understanding of the story. In the same way as we call our best friends after losing our job, or ending a relationship, to go over and pick apart the constituent elements that made up the job or relationship. This element of narrativisation creates yet another contradiction whereby to create a story as a whole object the narrative must be broken apart so the meaning of it can be revealed. The egg needs to break for the bird to be born. What this disassembly of narrative elements offers is a different form of finality than the mere material change offered by an ending, instead it offers closure.

Closure is often referred to with regards to finality, as it implies an ability to close a narrative. A relationship may have 'ended', for instance, but closure is needed for finality. This act of closing, just like opening, is a better fit for narrativisation than the mere requirement of an ending. Closing, again like opening, has agency and the moment of closure requires action, whereas endings, it is implied, simply happen. To close something, in both the literal and the metaphorical sense, requires effort, expenditure of energy, willingness and a level of control that an ending does not. Closure, in this respect, is *far* healthier and more productive than an ending. By disassembling the constituent parts of the narrative, we reach a close, typically long after the definitive ending. As such, we come to the conclusion that when it comes to narrative structure narratives: open, describe change and then close. In this way we are better able to see the subjectivity inherent in narrativisation and why a clear and well executed narrative is better for all while not ignoring the objective needs of a story.

In the next and final part, we will be looking more explicitly at how narrative is used in life as we know it today and what that means 'living forwards'.

As a side note: the explanation of narrative structure in these last three chapters should reveal the lie propagated by the news and social media of today that so actively seeks narrative, looking for where it may 'emerge' like a weed. Firstly, as I hope I have proved, narratives do not simply emerge, they are created and the best ones are shared and survive. Secondly, attempting to create narratives at their point of change (news media's stock in trade) is problematic at best, dangerous at worst. Only at a point of finality are such significant events, like those we are experiencing today, able to be disassembled, analysed and offered a close. Journalism, as it once was, did just that: gathered the evidence and separate elements, then created the narrative by disassembling them to discover the change. This was necessitated by the time frame in which news *used* to work. Newspapers were daily, newscasts on television and radio were often only once a day; this offered reporters more time to understand the events, to then report on them. With rolling news and social media today, these narratives are absent by necessity. Immediate yet concrete reportage is impossible as the events happen, there is no narrative yet, instead, this modern format relies heavily on opinion/biases i.e. pre-narratives (which we explored in the previous part). For this reason, at a time when narratives are so widely discussed, it is important we understand them better, so that we recognise a full narrative when presented with one and that immediacy does not equate to efficacy.

Part 5

Life

Chapter 1

My Story

Here's a story.

I have a favourite dream (I'm aware we've already discussed my dreams and how pointless it is retelling them but there is a point to this one too, I swear). The first time I had this dream was when I was about eight; I was wandering around an American neighbourhood in the dark and I was on a long suburban road when I just remember jumping and shooting off into the sky, flying low over the roofs of the houses. I still remember the stomach-churning dips and dizzying highs as I drifted into the cloudless night sky looking down at a blanket of twinkling lights above and below. Similar dreams kept me throughout my school years. Wonderful dreams of jumping from the roof of my hated school then bouncing from the floor and literally 'leaping tall buildings in a single bound' like my favourite comic-book hero. The best feeling was when I could slow my descent and felt all the blood lift to my head like when a plane is landing. Another favourite variant was when I was in a giant trampoline the size of a cathedral and I was leaping around in the air, plummeting to the soft and bouncy ground which would cannon me up again hundreds of feet up towards the ceiling. Like all dreams it's hard to explain the exhilaration, the joy, the unbounded freedom I felt as the wind rushed in my face and dried my eyes. It was always a wrench to wake up after one of those dreams.

Those dreams were so common and so enjoyable I even wrote a – now long lost – screenplay about them. I am still convinced it is possible for humans to fly, we just haven't evolved there yet. The feeling was so real and felt so natural that I was sure we either had the ability and lost it or will evolve to have it one day. I loved to watch films in which people fly, where it looks and feels like it did in my dreams.

On the day before my nineteenth birthday, I wanted to go up to London for the day and have a look for some music books, go to Denmark Street, drool over things I couldn't afford, generally enjoy a day on my own in the capital. I had also booked a ride on the Millennium Eye at sunset (it was still called that back when I went on it, which dates the story rather). I headed into town that day and was surprised to get a message from my father who then met me at Leicester Square. I'll never forget that. He was living elsewhere at the time and I can only imagine he had lots of work to do that day (being self-employed despite it being a Saturday) but whatever else there was he could have done, he came and met me and spent the whole day with me. That was the kind of father my dad was. He did everything he could for his kids. While we were out, he bought me some 'extra' birthday presents that I spotted, and he bought them saying he'd give them to me tomorrow. A few hours before sunset Dad asked if I wanted to go to the cinema because he knew I loved the movies. Of course, I said yes. We went back to Leicester Square and went into the Empire to see the Ang Lee movie *Hulk*.

That film got a lot of stick, but I enjoyed it; it's certainly more distinctive than a lot of the superhero fare around today. The ending was a little uninspired, though. Anyway, in the last third of the film, the Incredible Hulk is bounding across the Sierra Nevada away from pursuing helicopters, when out of nowhere... there it was. Flight as I had dreamed it. There's a shot where you see the Hulk jump from one giant stack of red rock in the desert and bound into the air. It then cuts to a shot of his face as he falls/flies. The wind ripples his hair and cheeks as his eyes close and the music stops and all you can hear is the rush of wind, cloud-dusted blue skies behind him. That was exactly what my dreams were like. It was at that moment my father leant over to me from the seat next to me and said simply:

'I can do that in my dreams.'

I had to watch the DVD to find out what happened immediately after that scene as I was so stunned by this I didn't pay attention. At the age of almost 19 I had never felt so close to my dad.

A little less than 2 years later, I was at Addenbrooke's Hospital in Cambridge sitting by my father's bed and staring out at the flatlands through the window. It was a spectacular view, we'd got very lucky with the care he received. He was on the NHS yet essentially had his own private room. Dad always said how much he loved the landscape of England, especially the Fens. Sitting there, it was a rare moment we had alone that week and I didn't say much to him then, just how I loved him and was going to miss him. I remember him waking up though, briefly, and staring out of the window at the flatlands. He didn't look at me, just out of the window at the view then went back to sleep. I hope he dreamed he was flying over those lush and verdant lands he loved so much before he died.

I haven't dreamed I was flying since.

That is a true story. Or for our purposes, it's a consistent narrative that has consensus. I'm a writer so there are admittedly some techniques and style choices in there that perhaps wouldn't occur if I were just relating it verbatim or as a spoken anecdote. In spite of that though, the above story is the truth.

Or is it?

The honest truth of the matter is that I am *presenting* the story as true because it is true *to me*. As difficult for me to acknowledge as it is, not only is it not important to anyone else (you may sympathise, in which case: thank you, but it does not affect your life in any real way) but the story in no way can be proved. I say it is consistent and it has consensus but the only person who could add testimony to the events of the story is my father and as you may have gathered…well…he's dead.

My dreams are solely in my head and, as we've established, aren't typically of interest to anyone except maybe a psychiatrist, though I think Freudian dream analysis is a thing of the past, so probably not even them. Perhaps if you could gather some sort of anecdotal evidence from other people who all say 'Yes, I dream I can fly too' we could establish a distant consensus. Then you could ask me lots of different questions about these dreams and (hopefully) my answers would remain consistent, though I can't guarantee that. My father died in 2005 which is already heavily reliant on memory as it was in the days before widespread social media and online archiving, and as such my memory of that time is pretty hazy by now. I also had most of those dreams 10 years prior to that. So there's nothing really to support my claim I had dreams of flying.

As to the trip to London before my birthday, I suppose we could check if the Empire has a schedule of all its showings over the last 20 years (unlikely). Working backwards, I reckon this would have been 2 August 2003. A quick web search says I'm right about it being a Saturday. I do have some photographs from the Millennium Eye looking at the sunset, but I don't think they're dated and I'm not even in them. I can't remember exactly what music books Dad bought me, but I still own plenty of music books that I suppose support the story. You might also be able to ask my mum and my housemate of the time to see if they remember me going so you could get a consensus that I did indeed go to London that day, but I can't prove we went to see *Hulk* and what happened when I was sat there watching it with Dad.

My father passed away in Addenbrooke's Hospital in Cambridge on 18 February 2005, there's proof of that. We have a death certificate, lots of people saw me there at the hospital with him, that part of the story, I'd argue, is irrefutable, but unfortunately the point of the end of the story is that I was alone with him. What I said and what I thought in that very brief moment of solitude before Uncle Ray (not my real uncle, I should clarify) came in and gave me a comforting pat on the shoulder, was not observed by anyone. Even the fact I have not dreamed I could fly since then has no consensus or proof. The best I can offer to this story is consistency, ask me any detail and – as far as my memory will allow – I can answer.

You might say, 'Well, what does this matter? This is your story and it is only important to you. If you say it's true, then it's true to you.' And this is precisely the point of this book. *All narratives are only true to you.* We can dig through archives and question people over whatever we like but an actual, solid, undisputable, objective 'truth' is hard to come by. This does not mean truth does not matter, it also does not mean there is no point trying to discover the truth; it does mean, however, that truth is a different thing to us than it is to someone else and it is all dependent on narrative. If the police are investigating a crime, they could have video evidence, DNA and ten witnesses to help them build a case against their suspect. This will help them ascertain with a high degree of certainty what happened, but it is still within some constraints. Video evidence can be tampered with, low resolution and a 'reading' of it can vary from person to person. DNA evidence, contrary to popular belief, is not infallible, and witnesses will bring their own narratives and bias to their testimony. We could poke holes in this all day but for the purposes of a healthy society all that evidence contributes to a consensus understanding of the crime which would be more than enough to convict. The takeaway from this should be that even something with 'hard evidence' is part of a narrative. The police construct the narrative through consensus and consistency from all the available evidence, they then *present that story as true.*

I present the story of me and my dad as true with very little hard evidence to support the narrative. I'm also leaving out 20 years of my dad and I's relationship. You, dear reader, probably have similar stories yourself, ones that cannot be objectively proved but that are integral to your own personal narrative, and to dismiss them now would be crushing. It's these narratives that make us who we are, that construct our identity and that is what we will be looking at further in the next chapter.

Chapter 2

Our Memory

In another poem by Yeats, he describes memory as:

... the mountain grass
Cannot but keep the form
Where the mountain hare has lain.

A potent image that shows the indelible and unintentional nature of memory, something that gets to the heart of our discussion.

I have avoided this subject so far because it is a pretty dense topic but it is also a fundamental part of building narratives, whether it is a personal one or a broader, cultural one. It's difficult to overstate the importance of memory in every facet of our lives but there are ways we are able to observe its significance, such as in those with memory issues. People with eidetic memory perfectly recall moments with astounding accuracy and detail. While generally we praise this in fiction as a positive trait (Sherlock Holmes, George Smiley and other fictional heroes are described as having perfect memories) in real life it could lead to or be part of hyperthymesia, the ability to perfectly remember and recall autobiographical details, which does not sound ideal to me. Equally, those with the fiction writer's favourite memory disorder, amnesia, are unlikely to discover they are in fact an ultra-competent spy/assassin and more likely to spend their life in need of constant care as we see in the tragic cases of those with Alzheimer's and other forms of dementia. Memory is essential to a functional existence and it is in memory that the seed of narrative grows. But while memory is essential, having perfect memory can be as much of a hindrance as not having one at all.

Sigmund Freud's research implied that the purpose of

memory is to forget. He was referring to the repression of trauma when in *The Psychopathology of Everyday Life* he said: 'We assert that besides the simple forgetting of proper names there is another forgetting which is motivated by repression' but we can extend this understanding of the need to forget to the healthy function of our minds as a whole. The inherent discretion the mind has to hold on to certain events as 'key' or developmental memories is the mental algorithm that creates narrative. Minds work as they do among the neurotypical due to the fact we must forget as much as we must remember. Unfortunately, memory is rarely under our control, similar to the way we move through time. Post-traumatic stress, for instance, is caused by the involuntary remembering of a traumatic event that has a myriad of unpleasant and punishing symptoms, both physical and mental. This lack of agency over memory is where we try to assert agency in the form of narrative. We deal with a trauma, for instance, by turning it into a story and relating our narrative of it to someone. We literally try and 'hand it over'. Josef Breuer, an associate of Freud's, adapted Aristotle's previously mentioned description of the purgation of emotion through art, catharsis, to relate to any method of 'release' for a deep emotion. This mode of catharsis is dependent on our ability to construct narratives around repressed memories or unconscious defence mechanisms just as we are able to build narratives out of happy and mundane memories.

In this way we can see how memory, despite being intrinsic to the past, is an essential element of the present. Repression, or a lack of catharsis, asserts itself on the present as mental and physical health disorders that can be crippling. While Marcel Proust may have coined the term, the author Mary Anne Evans (known by her pen name George Eliot) explored this idea of involuntary memory and catharsis in her novel *Middlemarch* decades earlier than he or Breuer. The following quote explores, in profound detail, memory's importance upon the present:

> Even without memory, the life is bound into one by a zone
> of dependence in growth and decay; but intense memory
> forces a man to own his blameworthy past. With memory
> set smarting liking a reopened wound, a man's past is not
> simply dead history, an outworn preparation of the present:
> it is not a repented error shaken loose from the life: it is a
> still quivering part of himself, bringing shudders and bitter
> flavours and tinglings of a merited shame.

Other than being an exquisite piece of prose, this extract
combines most of the elements we have discussed in this book.
We are dependent to that zone of growth and decay i.e. time/
entropy but transcend it when a moment – imbued with a
meaning that can be traumatic or otherwise – is returned to us
in the present, reopened like a wound, and affects our progress.
All of this is narrative. Driven by time, a story is made from
our memory, through necessity and from perception; given
life by narrative; which dictates our reality. Most importantly,
this equation interacts with others. Bulstrode's narrative of his
past is a 'still quivering part' of his present due to the dastardly
Raffles bringing his own greedy narrative along with him. In
this passage we vividly see the effect of narrative and not just on
the characters but the reader too.

Another example of how essential the narrative of memory is
to the present is in the 2000 film *Memento*. Two parallel stories
are told; one, shot in black and white, progresses forwards,
while the other, shot in colour, progresses backwards. This
creates the confusing effect of the narrative starting at the
'end'. This technique is employed to give the audience the same
understanding of events as the lead character who has anterograde
amnesia. His inability to create short-term memories means he
will forget what he is doing in the middle of the task. Unique in
cinema, this method of editing is used to deliberately make you
question every stage of the story but also shows the importance

of forward narrative to a cogent understanding of the world and ourselves. One of the biggest questions that hangs over *Memento* is the identity of the protagonist. For Guy Pearce in the lead role of Leonard, without a functioning memory, and for the audience without an awareness of where the story started, it is almost impossible to ascertain the 'truth' of the story or of Pearce's character even if we watch it the 'right' way round. This way of misusing traditional narrative structure and temporal reality is a common feature of director Christopher Nolan's work. His films serve to illustrate the importance of narrative integrity but equally where narrative is subjective. Just like memory.

Memento is also an excellent example of the necessity of consistency and consensus. The lack of memory for the protagonist and the audience shows us reality via consensus. Pearce's character must piece together his narrative with the help of other characters while the audience will do the same by discussing the outcome with others (or at least I did). It is a testament to memory's significance to narrative then that I still argue with people over the truth behind the identity of Pearce's enigmatic lead character. As the title implies, though, it is also an example of the need for consistency in narrative through evidence. Pearce's character tattoos his own body with 'facts', keeps the file of his wife's murder and takes instant photos of significant people or objects. This all, he thinks, contributes to a consistency in the narrative he has lost without a memory, but as we see, a lot of the evidence is manipulated, incomplete or just plain false. By the end we are none the wiser as to the who, the what, the where or the why of the story but acutely aware of its 'when'. *Memento* shows us how we must cement abstract concepts such as memory and time into narratives the way that we do, or we end up in an almost unliveable existence.

The impression of Yeats' hare upon the grass tells us where the animal was but as the full poem explores, it is that impression, that memory the grass holds, that can spell danger for it. The evidence the animal left behind is of great meaning to those that would hunt it and, for Yeats, a metaphor for the evidence of someone left behind that carries great meaning into the present.

These symbols and signs, discussions and debates are methods by which we settle upon our narratives in an objective world but narrative needs to be created around them or else they have no cohesion; they become untethered. The meanings we create for the signs, symbols and events in our lives need to be contextualised by narrative or they become pure abstraction that is impossible to grasp. Our reality depends on narrative, and narrative depends on memory. The significance of this abstract/ concrete interaction is, again, dependent on the meaning we imbue in these past events and the memories that add to this process.

The overarching theme of the above examples and our inability to separate meaning from the past due to memory can be summed up in the old adage 'forgive and forget'. This phrase perfectly encapsulates the intertwining of meaning and memory that serves us in everyday life and our need to engage with that memory to make sense of our present. Our ability to allow an event to become a 'past object' is dependent on our ability to choose its importance on the present. In Middlemarch, Bulstrode attempts to bury knowledge of his past life but his past reasserts itself on his present for precisely that reason; his lack of engagement with it. Whereas Leonard in Memento refuses to do anything *but* engage with his past, it has become his whole life, he literally carries it around with him wherever he goes. In both cases an ability to reconcile their past would give them the ability to forget, heal and live forwards. Because memory, due to its very presence, is always 'still quivering', narrative must respond to it. It is only when events, objects or people lose their significance that they can fall away from the narrative to be forgotten and vice versa. We cannot forgive if we cannot forget.

For the final chapter, now we understand the constituent

parts and the necessity of narrative, we will look at why this is so important in contemporary culture and where the current narrative leads us.

Chapter 3

The Narrative

Today, then.

We find ourselves in a world of deep division. Not just of the Left and Right or the Haves and Have-Nots, but in almost every part of society we see almost insurmountable breaks within groups. The poorest despising the poorest, the rich against the rich, nations at war with themselves, to say nothing of the rise of authoritarianism across the globe, resentment towards those fleeing persecution to seek safety abroad and a debate around climate change that has long since passed the need for debate. We are living through the foundational years of the twenty-first century, just as the First World War was the foundation upon which the twentieth was built. In the 19 years since the millennium we have seen global shifts of such a transformative nature the world is unrecognisable from what it was before 9/11 – because, let's be clear, that was certainly the fracture point (or the 'caesura'). The digital revolution (that has outstripped even the Industrial Revolution in terms of raw cultural restructuring), the 2008 crash, the 'Long 2016' and 9/11 have left the globe – and not just majority white or English-speaking countries – in a fundamentally altered state. It is a world without consistent narratives.

The reason the current oldest generation (the proudly self-styled 'Baby Boomers') believe theirs to be in some way more sensible and wiser than subsequent ones is because they were born at a time when there was a near singular, global narrative. Growing up after the single largest global conflict in history, that resulted in the deaths of approximately 60 million people for a cause still trumpeted today as clearly and unambiguously for the good of mankind, that generation inherited a narrative so strong, so consistent and with such overwhelming consensus that to transition to the fractured narratives of life in 2019 is understandably difficult. We can also see why narratives could be so consistent prior to the twenty-first century due to the control of information. News outlets were few and generally had to be more discerning about which stories they told, today news is constant and varied. With television channels now being dedicated to a 24-hour news cycle, hundreds of different blogs, social media and the so-called 'democratisation of opinion', video and on-demand streaming services and smart devices carried everywhere we go, the sheer volume of narratives bombarding the average person is impossible to sift through. Narratives have become currency, and the reason it is important to say 'narrative' and not simply 'news' is that all of this new information consists of both fact, opinion and pure fiction (both acknowledged and not). The result of this is that – just like we discussed in the retelling of history – we need to use our discretion to pick out which narratives we find relevant, but with the sheer volume being produced to meet market demand (not customer demand, to clarify) we have created technology that builds our narratives for us.

Many are the scare stories about computers that write novels (ignoring the fact those novels are universally unreadable) but few are the stories that point out we are already reading narratives written by computers. The almighty algorithm is seen as the solution to our problems of information saturation in the digital world, as you are able to streamline the recommendations wherever you go to receive stories that are important or relevant to you. Algorithms are essentially extremely fast ways of sifting through information to aggregate stories into a narrative solely for you. It is not pointed out that all algorithms are programmed and edited by people who, unintentionally or not, program them to have biases i.e. make them more like themselves or build them to the wishes of their business, because we might be more wary of them if that was better known. There's a reason it is called your search 'History', after all. Our news feeds, recommendations, advertising and search bars are all narratives given consistency and consensus by us. Where once our individual narratives only clashed with those around us, in our families and communities, algorithms are now fed these narratives we have created, they provide information to strengthen and solidify those narratives and then give us a way of finding others with similar narratives by giving us a platform on a global scale. Like most technology it is foolish to try and paint this as good or bad. I know I have benefitted hugely from the internet and the narrative generators of algorithms, but the result of this method of narrative curation has been that we have ended up in very entrenched groups. This technology has brought these smaller sub-sets of political and social groups together who then build up their narratives so – to them – they are utterly consistent and have total consensus. This phenomenon has been called various things, such as the 'echo chamber' of social media or 'group think', some go as far as to say 'cult', but none of us are free of it. Even if you proudly do not use the internet, traditional media (those that still exist) have been forced to compete, responding to viewers/readers input they must double down on certain narratives and foster their own niche market or suffer collapse.

One of the social narratives created to be a supposedly objective system is one that, in a very real sense, dictates our lives: the economic theory of 'The 'Market'. Derived from the notion that 'competition drives innovation' The Market is often presented as an infallible system whose 'forces' push its elements to interact with one another to see which one emerges as the strongest. Where once this may have been a visibly human interaction in a literal market place where those working the stalls continually altered their wares to better cater to the customer, this has been replaced by the insistence on the 'invisible hand' of trade in the global market place. This disingenuous narrative of The Market as some form of automata that thinks and feels for itself is a powerful one that has been seen as an indisputable, fundamental element of human society until very recently. The Market's power can, and is, being lessened by revealing it to be the construct of individuals in the financial and political system who benefit from its purported objective distance. This justification is what alienates those operating within it and dehumanises the population serving it. It is a shining example of how narrativisation based on even a flimsy premise (Adam Smith only used the phrase 'invisible hand' three times in his writing and never referred to 'The Market') can be utilised for control but also misrepresented as 'just the way things are'.

This leads us inexorably back to the examples of Elizabeth Warren and Rachel Dolezal from the introduction. The controversy surrounding them is based on the interpretation of heritage and race. Both created a narrative that came into conflict with the well-established narrative of race, but these stories also serve as an example that the idea of race is as much narrative as anything (I realise as a straight, white male from a wealthy country, my understanding and choice to speak on the subjects I am about to talk about is problematic and certainly lacking insight in many areas, but it is a point that must be reached when discussing narrativisation. Both its successes and its difficulties).

The topics that currently divide society most viciously, that create the most resentment, that foment outrage and even violence in seemingly every nation across the globe, are long held, long established, historically consistent and widely agreed upon narratives that are in the process of being overturned. Narratives of race, religion, gender, migration, climate, colonialism, even language itself are – thanks to the technologies and the awareness of the physics of existence we previously discussed – being rewritten, adjusted and newly presented. And let us be clear here, despite the understanding that narratives are fallible, abstract and difficult, that does not mean these new narratives can be dismissed. Lives depend on the restructuring of old narratives. *It has become a necessity that we better establish clear, consistent, consensus driven, global narratives.* If we continue our current model of splintering and dispersing groups, both figuratively and literally, we risk catastrophe. If you fully comprehended the size, scope and scale of climate change's impact there is nothing you wouldn't do to avert it, because it affects all of us, even those we assume may pass away before its worst effects are felt. So why does it create so much division? Because, despite all my discussion of history, entropy, consistency and consensus, while they all serve to illustrate the very real, practical effects narrative has on our objective reality, in spite of its seeming malleability, the 'truth' to narrative is its subjectivity.

Narrative, by the very nature of its origin in human perception, is subjective. It serves, first and foremost, our emotions. Practical appeals to heal divisions for the good of both sides, narratives that explain the necessity of the change required intelligently and with evidence, these narratives do not draw people to them. Since our earliest days, humanity's instinct is to gather around the fire, not simply for warmth but for the sense of community and to hear the stories of the day. At a time when communication is not only widely available but instant, the need to create narratives that draw us to a 'global hearth' should be simple, but instead of unifying it has divided. We are emotional, subjective beings so it is only through an understanding of our hopes and dreams, our fears and failures, our joy and sadness that we can hope to close the gaps in society as they currently exist. The way we can do this is through narrative.

I was dismissive earlier in this book of the Hegelian/Marxist claims of a grand narrative to the March of History. It is not consistent with the world or history, and despite declaring itself to be universal, it is decidedly anthropocentric in its vision, but it captures (and captures well) our desire for narrative in our lives and in society. Nationhood is the clearest example of this type of need we have for broader social and cultural narratives, but equally, with rising global migration and worrying shifts towards minority rule in some countries, we can see how that narrative is undergoing stress and need for change itself. While expressing a 'March of History' as an objective truth is misguided, it has the benefit of being a rallying point for progress. It helps gather together different narratives with different aims towards a common goal, a goal that may not be achievable, but an ideal, a Platonic 'Form' we can strive towards that benefits us all. It translates our desire for growth, development and change into an easily digestible narrative that is open enough to involve a diverse range of different beliefs and models for change. All through a single narrative.

We tell stories for a reason. To entertain, to inform, to educate, to control, to understand, to heal, to clarify, to unify. Narrative is at the very core of our being, it is how we arrange our lives, make sense of time, create our identity and understand others. In a very real way, we are just stories we tell each other, but it is in the telling, the presentation, of these stories that they become reality, it is where they take on their meaning. Whether it is the story of the latest blockbuster, a broken champagne flute, how I stopped dreaming I could fly, the story of someone's ethnic background, the history of a nation, your social media news feed, your memory of an important event, or just the lie you tell to get out of a commitment, we need these wild creatures in our lives. If the truth is that 'Life can only be understood backwards; but it must be lived forwards', then the better we 'understand backwards' and so the better we live today. Then, in turn, the key to 'living forwards', now narrative is better recognised, is to take great care in how we present our narratives, expect consistency and consensus in them, and ensure they retain the emotional core of their source.

That makes for a good story.

Postscript

Narrativisation is a pretty basic concept. 'We tell each other, and ourselves, stories' pretty much sums it up. Most of the concepts discussed in this book have been developed in more depth elsewhere, the Russian Formalist's theory of narratology is a good place to start if you wish to explore further. This book is an attempt to gather together disparate theories and philosophies that seem to be having such an effect on society today and hopefully make them more legible and approachable. They *are* all narratives after all.

I have done my best to generalise the discussion knowing how divisive contemporary analysis of almost any topic is and the near immediate criticism from those whose narratives differ. Unfortunately, no work is created in a vacuum and the context of this book's creation is certainly to be understood as being from a 'point of view'. While, as the author of this work, I may now be metaphorically 'dead' to it, it was certainly written with intent and a hope that it reaches as wide an audience as possible to assist with criticism of culture and our daily lives that is already so prevalent in the digital age. It also seems clear to me that narrativisation is already widespread enough that it is necessary to understand it better, so it is not allowed to fall into the sole possession of those I so profoundly disagree with. Because, for me, this would be a grievous error.

The danger we are presented with currently is that we are giving equal weight to narratives without consistency and renewing credence for narratives that have already been dismissed. The demand for 'free speech' that is ringing in our ears on a daily basis in the 'West' (whatever that is) today is a largely Right-leaning narrative that overwhelmingly favours an attempt to resurrect delegitimised narratives of the past, about such things as race supremacy and binary gender roles. 'Free speech', as the 'Intellectual Dark Web' would have it, is their narrative of oppression and is almost *purely* a future narrative. It relies on fear mongering and 'what ifs' about the future to persuade others into agreeing with them, but this narrative is entirely solipsistic. There is no consensus nor consistency in these narratives they peddle, that capitalist nations and their leaders should be allowed to do as they please with impunity and that white people are some sort of oppressed sub-class. These are narratives of pure emotion, pure subjectivity. They meet the needs of a troublingly misinformed minority, and so an *affected* consensus is drawn up from this fledgling support; it is then that what they believe passes for objective evidence is used to support these narratives in an attempt to create consistency. The trouble is, the evidence they use is singular, pulled out from the whole, recontextualised to fit their narrative. Evidence about evolutionary hierarchies and physiological studies of feminine frailties are plucked from their source narratives and put inside a story about men's needs and their rights; it doesn't matter that there is no causal link between the evidence and the pronouncement, it just looks like it fits. Even simply using dated references that have been disputed or discredited at large by more rigorous means can be used as historical evidence to provide consistency. The end result is that you have a narrative that is totally inconsistent, with a limited consensus but it can just about pass as a story object, to be presented to the world at large. Then you gather another equally flimsy narrative, like the one about freedom of speech being under threat on university campuses (also without any solid evidence), and this helps prop up other narratives, like the ones about white nationalism and there being only two genders etc. On and on this goes until you have a series of matchstick houses held together with spit, string and ill will. Yet these are the types of narratives that are *guiding the majority of discourse* in the media and online today. I do not wish to name names on this topic as the most obvious perpetrators of this method get far too much publicity as it is, but the dangers of this practice – to me at least – are obvious, immediate and real. The impact and harm of allowing bad faith narratives to grow is worryingly visible today. It is essential that those of us who wish to challenge these narratives and see our own narratives of the future borne out attempt a less fractured method of narrative creation.

Cards on the table, as a devout 'Lefty' I feel the need for better narrative use on the Left is essential and, sadly, lacking. *To have a successful movement towards significant change requires a consistent narrative that enables consensus and retains emotion.* On this point the Right – and their occasional, unintentional allies in the 'centre' – have us beat. They are able to create emotional narratives to give life to their stories and then organise around them far better than the Left are currently willing or able to do. Despite protestations of solidarity, consistency and consensus is absent in most of the Left's narratives today, and it is losing us ground to a highly mobilised, increasingly powerful Right. The Left, as we are all more than willing to point out, and with good intention, get bogged down in internal disputes that, while usually an attempt at clarification and inclusion, do result in poor optics. We look, and in some cases are, fractured and not unified. Our disputes are often legitimate, criticising the UK Labour Party for its mishandling of anti-Semitism is wholly valid for instance, but by allowing the narrative to be co-opted outside the Left and cynically overused to discredit the party is indicative of how poorly we understand presenting narratives, both good and bad. When we look at the successes of movements from history, they were able to create emotionally rich, evidence-based and widely agreed upon narratives that could subsume contrary ones, again, for both good and bad ends. We see this today in the way the global Right, despite being brazenly unpleasant and totally incompetent, is able to mop up supposedly 'moderate' conservatives and foster discord among the centre and the Left while equally being able to absorb elements of 'reasonable' centrist thinking. Right-wing leaders and parties across the world, far from appealing to the 'sensible, moderate voter', gain their support and control from leaning heavily into narratives of climate denial, race repression and delegitimising discussions over gender and sexuality, while also accommodating anyone favouring the individualist, neo-liberal consensus of the last 40 years or so. This commitment to narrative isn't fully adopted on the Left because it is, by its nature, exclusionary despite being 'populist', and that is generally not a compromise we are willing to accept.

The Left certainly have their narratives, but they tend to be disparate. Income inequality, poverty, reduction in global conflict, investment in modern technology, education, health care, all these and more are much needed narratives with clear, unambiguous messages but we tend to break into separate camps over how they should be achieved and to what extent. While understandable, it is frustrating to watch. We are not currently in control of the narrative because we are caught up in defining one.

I do not know the solution to this problem. I do not know what a grand, unifying narrative for the Left would look like, but I do feel that this *is* the root of the problem. At the very least, it is the aim of this book to bring awareness to our own agency when it comes to the issues facing the world in 2019. We are able to tell our own stories to the largest audience possible unlike we have ever been able to before. The reach of a popular YouTube video is greater than that of the Nuremburg Rallies (make of that what you will). Collectively, in my work for Wisecrack, my videos of critical readings of different intellectual properties have reached more people than have bought Bertrand Russell's books. That does not mean I am better, or my work has more intellectual value than Russell's, but it is proof that a more accessible narrative draws people to it and does not get buried in the saturated (and fictitious) 'free market place of ideas'.

The term 'influencer' is a recent one that refers to popular internet celebrities. Companies have recognised these people have a great deal of influence over their audience; this helps these companies and businesses work with these celebrities to market their products. The product is associated with the highly manufactured lifestyle these influencers project. While I find this practice distasteful, it makes clear the influence you can have on something as inconsequential as the sales of makeup or contact lenses just by adopting the right narrative. Again, here the Right were ahead of the game. They have had 'influencers' in place on social media for years and, woefully inept and utterly puerile as they may be, they have gathered support to the point that sites like Twitter, Facebook and YouTube – with the tacit blessing of the sites' owners themselves, no less – have become places where almost any posts that disagree with the Right-wing narrative are subjected to grotesque vitriol and abuse. The Left is catching up in this regard, with various internet personalities advocating for change, but we are still butting against the entrenched recontextualising by Right-wing 'influencers' of Left-wing ideas as wholly negative. The fact social justice has been repurposed to be a pejorative term seems ludicrous to me, but there are few insults that draw ire from the Extremely Online like the accusation of being an SJW (Social Justice Warrior) does today.

All hope is not lost of course, the Left actually has a presence today and is slowly gaining support and power, unlike in the last 40 years or so, but we have made it hard for ourselves. Those of us who wish to see progress and positive change globally (and not just for our individual nations) *far* outnumber those who resist it and, I believe, always will. But without similarly strong narratives, the kind that are so ably and quickly disseminated by the Right, the Left flounders. The stories we need to tell are important, essential even, but require a vast and wide-reaching consensus to enact. It is my hope that some 'influencers' on the Left are able to create narratives that help to unify the disparate factions and help us 'live forwards' into a more prosperous future and 'understand backwards' that these times were, as a wise man once said: 'but the passing of greed'.

Please. Tell your story.

CULTURE, SOCIETY & POLITICS

The modern world is at an impasse. Disasters scroll across our smartphone screens and we're invited to like, follow or upvote, but critical thinking is harder and harder to find. Rather than connecting us in common struggle and debate, the internet has sped up and deepened a long-standing process of alienation and atomization. Zer0 Books wants to work against this trend.

With critical theory as our jumping off point, we aim to publish books that make our readers uncomfortable. We want to move beyond received opinions.

Zer0 Books is on the left and wants to reinvent the left. We are sick of the injustice, the suffering and the stupidity that defines both our political and cultural world, and we aim to find a new foundation for a new struggle.

If this book has helped you to clarify an idea, solve a problem or extend your knowledge, you may want to check out our online content as well. Look for Zer0 Books: Advancing Conversations in the iTunes directory and for our Zer0 Books YouTube channel.

Popular videos include:

Žižek and the Double Blackmain

The Intellectual Dark Web is a Bad Sign

Can there be an Anti-SJW Left?

Answering Jordan Peterson on Marxism

Follow us on Facebook
at https://www.facebook.com/ZeroBooks and Twitter at
https://twitter.com/Zer0Books

Bestsellers from Zer0 Books include:

Give Them an Argument
Logic for the Left
Ben Burgis
Many serious leftists have learned to distrust talk of logic. This is a
serious mistake.
Paperback: 978-1-78904-210-8 ebook: 978-1-78904-211-5

Poor but Sexy
Culture Clashes in Europe East and West
Agata Pyzik
How the East stayed East and the West stayed West.
Paperback: 978-1-78099-394-2 ebook: 978-1-78099-395-9

An Anthropology of Nothing in Particular
Martin Demant Frederiksen
A journey into the social lives of meaninglessness.
Paperback: 978-1-78535-699-5 ebook: 978-1-78535-700-8

In the Dust of This Planet
Horror of Philosophy vol. 1
Eugene Thacker
In the first of a series of three books on the Horror of Philosophy,
In the Dust of This Planet offers the genre of horror as a way of
thinking about the unthinkable.
Paperback: 978-1-84694-676-9 ebook: 978-1-78099-010-1

The End of Oulipo?
An Attempt to Exhaust a Movement
Lauren Elkin, Veronica Esposito
Paperback: 978-1-78099-655-4 ebook: 978-1-78099-656-1

Capitalist Realism
Is There no Alternative?
Mark Fisher
An analysis of the ways in which capitalism has presented itself as
the only realistic political-economic system.
Paperback: 978-1-84694-317-1 ebook: 978-1-78099-734-6

Rebel Rebel
Chris O'Leary
David Bowie: every single song. Everything you want to know,
everything you didn't know.
Paperback: 978-1-78099-244-0 ebook: 978-1-78099-713-1

Kill All Normies
Angela Nagle
Online culture wars from 4chan and Tumblr to Trump.
Paperback: 978-1- 78535-543-1 ebook: 978-1-78535-544-8

Cartographies of the Absolute
Alberto Toscano, Jeff Kinkle
An aesthetics of the economy for the twenty-first century.
Paperback: 978-1-78099-275-4 ebook: 978-1-78279-973-3

Malign Velocities
Accelerationism and Capitalism
Benjamin Noys
Long listed for the Bread and Roses Prize 2015, *Malign Velocities*
argues against the need for speed, tracking acceleration
as the symptom of the ongoing crises of capitalism.
Paperback: 978-1-78279-300-7 ebook: 978-1-78279-299-4

Meat Market
Female Flesh under Capitalism
Laurie Penny
A feminist dissection of women's bodies as the fleshy fulcrum of
capitalist cannibalism, whereby women are both consumers and
consumed.
Paperback: 978-1-84694-521-2 ebook: 978-1-84694-782-7

Babbling Corpse
Vaporwave and the Commodification of Ghosts
Grafton Tanner
Paperback: 978-1-78279-759-3 ebook: 978-1-78279-760-9

New Work New Culture
Work we want and a culture that strengthens us
Frithjoff Bergmann
A serious alternative for mankind and the planet.
Paperback: 978-1-78904-064-7 ebook: 978-1-78904-065-4

Romeo and Juliet in Palestine
Teaching Under Occupation
Tom Sperlinger
Life in the West Bank, the nature of pedagogy and the role of a
university under occupation.
Paperback: 978-1-78279-637-4 ebook: 978-1-78279-636-7

Ghosts of My Life
Writings on Depression, Hauntology and Lost Futures
Mark Fisher
Paperback: 978-1-78099-226-6 ebook: 978-1-78279-624-4

Sweetening the Pill
or How We Got Hooked on Hormonal Birth Control
Holly Grigg-Spall
Has contraception liberated or oppressed women?
Sweetening the Pill breaks the silence on the dark side of hormonal
contraception.
Paperback: 978-1-78099-607-3 ebook: 978-1-78099-608-0

Why Are We The Good Guys?
Reclaiming your Mind from the Delusions of Propaganda
David Cromwell
A provocative challenge to the standard ideology that Western
power is a benevolent force in the world.
Paperback: 978-1-78099-365-2 ebook: 978-1-78099-366-9

The Writing on the Wall
On the Decomposition of Capitalism and its Critics
Anselm Jappe, Alastair Hemmens
A new approach to the meaning of social emancipation.
Paperback: 978-1-78535-581-3 ebook: 978-1-78535-582-0

Enjoying It
Candy Crush and Capitalism
Alfie Bown
A study of enjoyment and of the enjoyment of studying. Bown asks
what enjoyment says about us and what we say about enjoyment,
and why.
Paperback: 978-1-78535-155-6 ebook: 978-1-78535-156-3

Color, Facture, Art and Design
Iona Singh
This materialist definition of fine-art develops guidelines for
architecture, design, cultural-studies and ultimately social change.
Paperback: 978-1-78099-629-5 ebook: 978-1-78099-630-1

Neglected or Misunderstood
The Radical Feminism of Shulamith Firestone
Victoria Margree
An interrogation of issues surrounding gender, biology, sexual-
ity, work and technology, and the ways in which our imaginations
continue to be in thrall to ideologies of maternity and the nuclear
family.
Paperback: 978-1-78535-539-4 ebook: 978-1-78535-540-0

How to Dismantle the NHS in 10 Easy Steps (Second Edition)
Youssef El-Gingihy
The story of how your NHS was sold off and why you will have to
buy private health insurance soon. A new expanded second edition
with chapters on junior doctors' strikes and government blueprints
for US-style healthcare.
Paperback: 978-1-78904-178-1 ebook: 978-1-78904-179-8

Digesting Recipes
The Art of Culinary Notation
Susannah Worth
A recipe is an instruction, the imperative tone of the expert, but this constraint can offer its own kind of potential. A recipe need not be a domestic trap but might instead offer escape – something to fantasise about or aspire to.
Paperback: 978-1-78279-860-6 ebook: 978-1-78279-859-0

Most titles are published in paperback and as an ebook.
Paperbacks are available in traditional bookshops. Both print and ebook formats are available online.
Follow us on Facebook
at https://www.facebook.com/ZeroBooks
and Twitter at https://twitter.com/Zer0Books